Black Drink

Black Drink

A Native American Tea

Charles M. Hudson, Editor

THE UNIVERSITY OF GEORGIA PRESS

ATHENS

University of Georgia Press paperback edition, 2004
© 1979 by the University of Georgia Press
Athens, Georgia 30602
All rights reserved

Set in 10 on 12 point Linotype Baskerville
Printed digitally

Printed in the United States of America

The Library of Congress has cataloged the hardcover
edition of this book as follows:
Black drink : a native American tea / Charles M. Hudson,
editor.
175 p. : ill. ; 22 cm.
Bibliography: p. [166]–170.
Includes index.
ISBN 0-8203-0462-x
Contents: Hu, S.Y. The botany of yaupon.—Merrill,
W.L. The beloved tree, Ilex vomitoria among the Indians
of the Southeast and adjacent regions.—Milanich, J.T.
Origins and prehistoric distributions of black drink and
the ceremonial shell drinking cup.—Fairbanks, C.H. The
function of black drink among the Creeks.—Sturtevant,
W.C. Black drink and other caffeine-containing beverages
among non-Indians.

1. Black drink. 2. Indians of North America—Food—
Southern States. 3. Ilex vomitoria. I. Hudson, Charles M.
E78.S65 B58   641.3'37   78-18751

Paperback edition: ISBN 0-8203-2696-8

Contents

Maps

Illustrations

Preface

This book had its beginning in a classroom at the University of North Carolina, Chapel Hill, in the summer of 1971. I had been lecturing on biack drink, and in discussing it after class with two students, William Merrill and Harold Cable, who were then undergraduates, we decided that it would be worthwhile for the three of us to put together a paper on the subject. This we presented as "The Black Drink of the Southeastern Indians" at the nineteenth annual meeting of the American Society for Ethnohistory in Athens, Georgia, in October 1971.

The paper stimulated more interest and discussion than we had anticipated. We learned that there was far more to be known about black drink than we had uncovered. After the session we got together with Charles Fairbanks, William Sturtevant, and Jerald Milanich, all of whom had been in the audience, and with Kenneth Cherry, then representing the University of Georgia Press. We anthropologists discovered that we all had a long-standing interest in black drink, that we had notes and bibliographies tucked away in our files, and that our ideas on the subject were complementary but not necessarily overlapping. We decided to put forth a joint effort and to produce a collection of papers on the subject.

I gratefully acknowledge an appointment in the Institute for Behavioral Research at the University of Georgia, where I did initial editing, and a fellowship at the Center for the History of the American Indian, the Newberry Library, where I did final editing.

C.H.

Introduction

Charles Hudson

Having taught for several years at the University of Georgia a course on the Indians of the southeastern United States, I know that it rarely surprises anyone that the Indians of the Southeast made a tea from the leaves and twigs of Yaupon holly (*Ilex vomitoria* Ait.). What does come as a surprise is that this native holly is widely used as an ornamental shrub in the Southeast. Even more surprising, the active ingredient of the tea that is made from it—caffeine—and its mildly bitter taste make it a beverage closely comparable to coffee and Asian tea. So close, in fact, that if coffee and Asian tea for some reason became unavailable or too expensive, this tea of the south-eastern Indians could easily be used as a substitute. In southern Brazil, Chile, Argentina, Uruguay, and Paraguay, *maté*, a caf-feinated beverage made from the leaves of a holly (*Ilex para-guariensis* St.-Hil.), is used as an alternative, by many a preferred alternative, to coffee and Asian tea. Why, we may ask, is this southeastern Indian tea not more generally known? And we may again ask the question first asked by Edwin M. Hale in 1891: why is it not drunk by Americans today just as tea, coffee, chocolate, and *maté* are still drunk in those parts of the world where they were first developed?[1]

The truth about this native tea is so beclouded by faulty knowledge that the best way to begin a detailed examination of it is first to set forth some plain facts and then to explain step by step how these facts have been distorted and misrepresented. In standard ethnological works on the southeastern Indians, yaupon tea is often called "cassina," an Anglicized version of an Indian (probably Timucuan) name for the beverage, or even more commonly, "black drink," a name derived from the fact that in making it the Indians boiled the parched yaupon leaves and twigs until they had a strong decoction, quite dark in color.

The native habitat of yaupon holly is along the Atlantic coast from Virginia down to central Florida and along the Gulf coast from central Florida around to southern Texas. Hence, yaupon grows primarily within the southeastern culture area, although its range does extend outside the Southeast both to the northeast and to the southwest. As William Merrill shows in the third chapter of this volume, historical evidence suggests that all the Indians of the Southeast probably used black drink, with the exception of some of the Indians along the Gulf coast and along the middle course of the Mississippi River. One suspects, however, that the seeming absence of black drink among these groups is due either to incomplete documentation or to a disruption of aboriginal patterns before the first European observers arrived. Although black drink was used by Indians outside the Southeast, its most elaborate use was by the southeastern Indians. In standard anthropological accounts of the southeastern Indians, black drink is one of their defining cultural traits. Invariably these accounts note that the Indians drank black drink for the purpose of causing themselves to vomit. But, as we shall see, describing black drink as essentially an emetic describes it incompletely and probably erroneously.

Going further, we would be justified in terms of our own categories of understanding in saying that the southeastern Indians drank black drink for three different purposes: (1) as a stimulating social beverage, much as we drink coffee or tea, although not so casually as we; (2) as a medicine to improve their physiological and psychological well-being; and (3) possibly as an emetic, to induce vomiting. The southeastern Indians themselves, however, probably would have said that they used black drink for a single purpose. Namely, it was drunk by adult males of high social standing in order to attain ritual purity. Consistent with this, some southeastern Indians called it "white drink," white being the symbolic color of peaceable men meeting in council. These symbolic values are discussed by Charles Fairbanks in the fifth chapter of this volume, in which he examines the use of black drink by the Creek Indians.

The notion of "purity" among the southeastern Indians can only be described as the tip of an ideological iceberg. It would be impossible to explain the full extent of it. meaning in a brief scope. Perhaps it is enough to say that the southeastern Indians went to great lengths to keep themselves in a ritually pure condition. This was particularly true of men. Ritual purity depended in part on the careful observance of certain rules of categorical separation and integrity. Some of these rules specified the eating of proper food. People were to eat the food appropriate to people, and animals were to eat the food appropriate to animals. And of the food appropriate to people, certain kinds of food were too impure to be eaten by adult males. Perhaps the most important categorical distinction in the world view of the southeastern Indians was that which existed between the sexes. Males, they believed, were especially likely to become impure through exposure to a menstruating female. Even to eat a bite of food prepared or touched by a menstruating woman would render a man impure, and in this condition any business he undertook was bound to fail. Furthermore, there was always a danger that food that was otherwise fit to eat had been mystically contaminated by witches or other ill sorts. It is by taking all of this into account that we may begin to understand their use of black drink to attain purity. It is likely that their drinking it before meeting in council with other men served to separate them ritually from women. And it is likely that they induced vomiting to rid themselves of any possible contamination by impure food.[2]

Deliberately induced vomiting was practiced not only by the southeastern Indians but by many other Indians in both North and South America. They used virtually every device known to modern medicine, including the simple expedient of sticking a finger down the throat. The puzzling thing about black drink is that it did not always induce vomiting. The Indians sometimes drank it for hours at a time as a social beverage, without vomiting. European traders and government officials who had dealings with the Indians in the eighteenth century drank it in this fashion in company with the Indians, and they did not vomit.

Just why black drink was an emetic in some cases and not in others is not at all clear. One suspects that the Indians may have sometimes added substances other than yaupon leaves to the decoctions they drank; European observers would not necessarily have noticed their doing so. In general, the southeastern Indians' understanding of plants and their uses was far more informed and extensive than was that of most of the Europeans who had dealings with them. Moreover, there is some evidence that Europeans used the terms "black drink" and "cassina" to refer to beverages made of other substances that were emetic—button snakeroot medicine, for example. Another possible explanation is that holly leaves contain small amounts of ilicin, ilicic acid, and chlorogenic acid, these being turpentinelike substances that can cause emesis.[3] When black drink was consumed in large quantities, particularly after fasting, these substances might have reached critical levels. Another possibility is that it was the act of suddenly drinking a large quantity of the hot beverage which caused emesis, an effect that can be achieved by simply drinking a large quantity of hot water. A further possibility is that with vomiting playing such a frequent role in the lives of southeastern Indian men, they may have acquired the ability to induce it by an act of will.

Whatever may have been the cause of the vomiting, the fact remains that when drunk in small quantities, like tea or coffee, black drink is not an emetic. But because we are all too ready to emphasize the bizarre and the exotic in the cultural practices of the Indians, black drink has become linked, one to one, to the southeastern Indians' inexplicable urge to vomit, and not only to vomit, but to do it copiously and in the company of their fellows. It is a drink of savages. Thus it was that after monumental terminological confusion (discussed in detail by Shiu Ying Hu in the second chapter of this volume), botanists

settled upon the name *Ilex vomitoria*. Not a good trade name
for a tea. As Merritt L. Fernald and Alfred C. Kinsey have
pointed out, this unappealing designation is completely unde-
served.[4]

Related to our emphasis on the bizarre elements in Indian
culture is our inclination to look more on the religious and
magical side of the Indians than on their rational and practical
side. We are all too familiar, therefore, with their use of such
mind-altering substances as peyote, psilocybin mushrooms, and
jimsonweed. But the fact is, the southeastern Indians, so far as
I have been able to determine, made little use of hallucinogens;
if they did, early European observers made no note of it. Black
drink, however, was not without its side effects. Its active ingredient, caffeine, is the only true cortical stimulant known to
modern medicine.[5] It is a most effective stimulant, exciting the
central nervous system at all levels, especially the cerebral cor-
tex. It heightens appreciation of sensory stimuli, produces a
clearer and more rapid flow of thought (I drink coffee as I
write this), shortens motor reaction time, strengthens skeletal
muscles, and lessens susceptibility to fatigue. It also has a mild
diuretic effect, causing perspiration. These effects are pro-
nounced with doses of 0.5 to 1.0 grams—the equivalent of
three to six cups of coffee. Of all the species of holly which are
native to North America, only yaupon is known to contain
caffeine. In discovering the stimulating properties of yaupon
holly, the southeastern Indians discovered what was perhaps
the only naturally occurring source of caffeine in their environment. Furthermore, they perfected the most effective means of
extracting maximum amounts of caffeine from the leaves. To
make the caffeine soluble in water they roasted the leaves (we
roast coffee beans for the same reason); and to maximize the
absorption of caffeine into their systems they drank the tea
while it was quite hot, the absorption level of caffeine being
approximately thirty times higher in boiling water than in
water at room temperature.[6] Our most up-to-date information
about how to use caffeine effectively adds little to the southeastern Indians' own traditional knowledge of its use.

It is not known with certainty when black drink was first used in the Southeast. As Charles Fairbanks points out in his chapter, the very thoroughness with which it was incorporated into Creek culture and social life is indirect evidence of a considerable antiquity. But as may be seen in Jerald Milanich's chapter, archaeology provides more tangible if not decisive evidence of the antiquity of black drink. The act of brewing and drinking a beverage does not leave any trace in the earth which can be discovered by an archaeologist. But from sixteenth-, seventeenth-, and eighteenth-century historical evidence, we know that black drink was commonly drunk from cups made from large marine shells that were collected on the Atlantic and Gulf coasts and traded to Indians in the interior—that the cups originate in the same coastal area where *Ilex vomitoria* thrives is probably not coincidental. These shell drinking cups are extremely durable. If we can take their presence in archaeological sites as an indication that black drink was being consumed, then we have reason to believe that black drink has a considerable antiquity. In South America the evidence for the prehistoric use of a holly with caffeine content is more direct. A burial was discovered in Bolivia of a medicine man who was interred with his paraphernalia, including some leaves of *Ilex guayusa*, a caffeine-bearing holly. This burial has been dated to about 500 A.D.[7]

One of the puzzles about black drink, or cassina, is why we do not drink it today. The Spanish colonists in Florida drank cassina perhaps as early as the sixteenth century, and subsequently it became very popular among them. They called it *té del indio* or *chocolate del indio*. It was taken to Europe at an early date. In England the imported leaves were made into a beverage called South-Sea tea. And in both England and North Carolina the beverage was called yaupon tea, Appalachian tea, and Carolina tea. In South Carolina, as in Spanish Florida, it was called cassina. In France it was called *Apalachine* or *Apalachina*, perhaps after the Apalachee Indians.

In Europe cassina lost out in competition with coffee, chocolate, and Asian tea. It met the same fate in North America.

Yet in South America the holly tea *maté* continues to be used as an alternative to coffee or tea. As E. M. Hale wrote in 1891, it was not that the taste of cassina was disagreeable to Europeans.

This infusion, if boiled for half an hour, gives a dark liquid like very strong black tea, of an aromatic odor, *sui generis*, not like coffee, but more like an Oolong tea without its pleasant rose odor. The taste is like that of an inferior black tea, quite bitter, but with little delicacy of flavor. It is not an unpleasant beverage, and I can imagine that the palate would become accustomed to it, as to maté, tea, or coffee.[8]

The demise of cassina, therefore, was not necessarily caused by a judgment of the European palate. It was far more likely caused by the economic pressures of tea and coffee merchants and, as a reflex of this, the tastes and conventions of social class. Cassina was so abundant on the coast that it could be drunk by the poor; hence it became déclassé. We find, therefore, that in the American South people who were too poor to afford coffee and tea continued drinking cassina. This was probably especially true during the Civil War, when the South had to make do with what was close at hand. But after the war, coffee and tea again became available and cassina declined in popularity. It continued to be used, however, in restricted areas along the Carolina coast as a folk or local color beverage. As William C. Sturtevant notes in the sixth chapter, the factors that led to the decline of cassina are complex. A full understanding of it would require concerted research by a social historian.

In addition to this historical problem, there are a number of other questions that require additional study. So far as I am aware, no research on variations in the caffeine content of *Ilex vomitoria* has been done since the paper of Frederick B. Power and Victor K. Chestnut in 1919. As Charles Fairbanks points out, the Creeks believed that yaupon came into prime in early or middle summer, when the plant puts forth new growth. The limited samples analyzed by Power and Chestnut suggest that the tender leaves picked in summer would have contained significantly higher levels of caffeine than old leaves or leaves picked in the fall and winter.[9] But more definitive research is needed. It would also be interesting to learn whether the caffeine content of *Ilex vomitoria* varies with soil conditions and other features of the various locations where it grows. Is the caffeine content of the yaupon that grows along the coast different from that which grows inland? This could shed light on Fairbanks's question of whether the southeastern Indians who lived in the interior procured yaupon by trade from the coast, planted and harvested their own, or did both.

Lastly, more chemical and pharmacological research ought to be done on how *Ilex vomitoria* might have been used to induce emesis. This could answer some of the lingering questions we have about its use by the Indians. And it could clear the way for any future attempts to produce and market cassina as a commercial tea.

The purpose of this volume is not to present a case for the marketability of cassina nor to answer every question that might arise concerning *Ilex vomitoria*. Rather, its purpose is to clear away the extraordinary confusion about an important ethnobotanical and ritual complex among the Indians of the Southeast and to describe the true nature of a caffeinated beverage that has so far failed to win an enduring place in Euro-American cuisine. Why this failure occurred still awaits full explanation but it seems dubious that it was because of some intrinsic property of parched *Ilex vomitoria* leaves. It is clear—if I may be allowed to play upon the words of Claude Lévi-Strauss—that cassina has always been both good for drinking and good for thinking.

NOTES

1. Edwin M. Hale, "Ilex Cassine: The Aboriginal North American Tea," U.S.D.A. Division of Botany Bulletin no. 14 (Washington, 1891), pp. 7, 13.

2. Charles Hudson, "Vomiting for Purity: Ritual Emesis in the

Aboriginal Southeastern United States," in Carole Hill, ed., *Symbols and Society: Essays on Belief Systems in Action*, Southern Anthropological Society Proceedings, no. 9 (Athens: University of Georgia Press, 1975), pp. 93–102; *The Southeastern Indians* (Knoxville: University of Tennessee Press, 1976), pp. 317–75.

3. Harold Cable, Charles Hudson, and William Merrill, "The Black Drink of the Southeastern Indians," paper presented at the 1971 meeting of the American Society for Ethnohistory, p. 12.

4. Merritt C. Fernald and Alfred C. Kinsey, *Edible Wild Plants of Eastern North America* (New York: Harper, 1958), p. 263.

5. Frederick B. Power and Victor K. Chestnut, "Ilex Vomitoria as a Native Source of Caffeine," *Journal of the American Chemical Society* 41 (1919): 1307–12.

6. Cable et al., "Black Drink," pp. 13–14. There is some evidence that caffeine is detrimental to health; see H. Leon Abrams, Jr., "Caffeine—A Paradigm of Subliminal Cultural Drug Habituation," *Journal of Applied Nutrition* 28 (1976): 33–40.

7. S. H. Wassen, ed., *A Medicine Man's Implements and Plants in a Tiahuanacoid Tomb in Highland Bolivia*, Etnologiska Studier 32 (Göteborg: Göteborgs Etnografiska Museum, 1972).

8. Hale, "Ilex cassine," p. 12.

9. Power and Chestnut, "Ilex vomitoria," p. 1310.

The Botany of Yaupon

Shiu Ying Hu

Yaupon differs from other American hollies in its general habit, its branching system, its leaves, the arrangement and structure of its flowers, and in its fruit and seed. Yaupon is an evergreen shrub that is adapted for the harsh life of semi-xeric conditions of the seashore and is adapted to a far lesser extent for the sterile bluffs of inland rivers. At sea level it grows on dunes, in hammocks, on the border of live-oak woods or pine woods, and on top of wooded bluffs above the shore. It is common in shore vegetation along creeks. It rarely occurs inland. When it does, it grows on exposed flood plains or on high, dry rocky bluffs. In general the species appears as shrubs 2–4 m. high. Small trees 7–10 m. high have been reported by L. Lakela at Turtle Mound Monument, Volusia County, Florida, and by C. C. Compten in Natchez, Mississippi. One observer reported that the trunk attains 7 cm. in diameter, with smooth, light gray bark.

Branch System. The typically barren growing condition of the species has an interesting effect on its branch system. A plant growing in its natural habitat has three types of shoots (see fig. 1a): the offshoot, the long shoot, and the short shoot. Plants grown in gardens do not have the distinctive short shoots.

An offshoot is a branch which develops from a dormant bud situated near the base of the major stem. It is rather stout and long, measuring 50–100 cm. in length and 3–4 mm. in diameter. It bears a terminal bud and may continue to elongate for several consecutive years. Its axillary buds may develop into lateral shoots on the second year growth. This type of shoot contributes to the vegetative function of the plant, and it seldom produces flowers and fruits.

A long shoot is one which develops from a strong axillary bud. It bears a terminal bud which produces a vegetative branch. A short shoot is one which develops from a weak axillary bud. It often bears no terminal bud, and when its leaves fall off, to a casual observer, it appears to be a thorn.

The annual growth of a long shoot varies from 3 to 8 cm. It contains from 6 to 12 nodes. The internodes are 2–10 mm. long, slightly angular, and rather densely covered by straight short hairs. The terminal and the axillary buds are roundish and covered by hairy scales which are persistent. It is by these scales or their scars that one can tell the length of the annual addition of the shoot.

The specialization in structure and function of the buds is a constant character of yaupon. On a mature plant, the terminal bud of a shoot is always a vegetative bud which develops into a leafy shoot, and the axillary buds develop into flower clusters or abbreviated shoots. The axillary buds of a juvenile offshoot develop into vegetative shoots, as does the terminal bud of a mature shoot.

Leaves. A spontaneous population of yaupon exhibits a wide range of variation in leaf size and shape. Variation exists among different leaves at various positions on a shoot, among different shoots on the same plant, among different individuals of a single population, and among the populations of an area.

In general the leaves are oblong, oblong-elliptic, or ovate-oblong; and they are 1–4 cm. long, 8–18 mm. wide, rounded or obtuse at the base, obtuse at the apex, and crenulate-serrate along the margin (fig. 1a). Each marginal tooth is terminated by a callose mucro which becomes black on drying and is visible under a hand lens. The upper surface is shiny green, and the lower one is pale and smooth. The petioles are short, varying from 2 to 3 mm. in length, and they are hairy like the young stem bearing them. The midrib of each leaf is evident on both surfaces, and the lateral nerves (4–5 on each side) are

Figure 1. The growing habit and male flowers of *Ilex vomitoria*. **a.** The habit sketch of a fruiting specimen showing the branching system with long and short shoots and axillary fascicles of globose fruits (Georgetown, S.C., Tarbox 22, × 1). **b, c, d.** Sections of fruiting branches of three plants showing the variation of the sizes and shapes of the leaves. **b.** A form with large leaves growing on sand dune (Georgetown, S.C., Godfrey and Tryon 652, × 1). **c.** A form with proportionally narrower, ovate-elliptic leaves (Florida, Harbison 10, × 1). **d.** A form with very small oblong leaves growing in salt marshes (Florida, Cooley and Eaton 6413, × 1). **e.** A male inflorescence showing an axillary fascicle consisting of 6 cymes and a central sterile portion with scales; the number of flowers per cyme variable; 1 cyme with 4 flowers, 2 cymes with 3 flowers, 1 cyme with 2 flowers, and 2 cymes with 1 flower (Florida, Faxon 1888, × 4). **f.** A single male cyme with 3 flowers showing the central position of the first opened flower, the 4 large oblong anthers, and the small pulvinate-subconic rudimentary ovary (Faxon 1888, × 9). **g.** The lateral view of a rotate corolla showing a very short tube, 4 large oblong lobes, and the stamens attached to the corolla tube and falling with it (Faxon 1888, × 9).

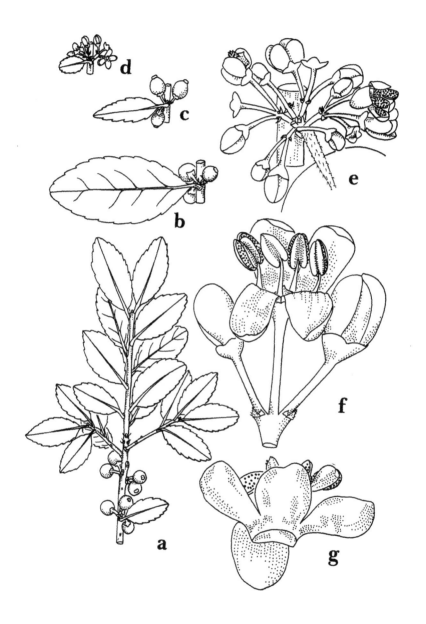

evident above but obscure beneath. Normally the leaves remain on the second year's stem. On offshoots functional leaves may remain on the third year's growth. On flowering branches the leaves usually drop off when the fruits of the axillary cluster reach mature size.

On a shoot the earlier leaves, which are situated at the basal portion of the year's growth, are smaller than the later ones, which are higher up on the shoot. The leaves of a juvenile offshoot are usually about twice the size of those on the flowering and fruiting shoots. The removal of leaves or leafy shoots stimulates the growth of offshoots, which consequently produce larger leaves.

Variations in the size and shape of leaves among individual plants are more striking than variations on the same plant (fig. 1b,c,d). Some plants have large oblong leaves measuring 3–4.5 cm. long and 1.5–2.5 cm. wide, while others have small ones measuring 7–15 mm. long and 3–8 mm. wide. Specimens from the Gulf coast of Florida exhibit the widest range of variation of leaf size and form. It is worthy of note that in regard to the size and shape of leaves, the specimens from disjunct areas of the coast of the Carolinas and Georgia, of Bermuda, and of the sterile bluffs along the inland rivers in a very limited region in the Ouachita Mountains in western Arkansas and southeastern Oklahoma are indistinguishable.

Flowers. The flowers of yaupon are dioecious; that is, the male and female flowers are produced by different plants. These male and female flowers differ from each other in arrangement, structure, and function. They are small and white, with the males ones more showy than the female.

In holly literature the arrangement of flowers on a plant is known as *inflorescence,* and the arrangement of fruits is known as *infrutescence.* The inflorescence of yaupon is fasciculate, with each fascicle consisting of many flowers. The fascicles appear in the axils of leaves on the second year's growth and on older branchlets. Morphologically a fascicle of yaupon is a specialized shoot developed from a flower bud. A male fascicle bears many more flowers than a female one.

A male fascicle of yaupon has secondary flower clusters (fig. 1 e,f). Each of these clusters consists of 1 to 5 flowers, and it is a unit of the fascicle. Basically a unit of a male fascicle is a 3-flowered cyme with the first opened flower situated at the middle (fig. 1f). Through multiplication or reduction, some cymes in a fascicle may have as many as 5 flowers while others are 1-flowered.

A female fascicle of yaupon consists of 1 to 7 flowers (fig. 2a). Female fascicles of 3 or 4 flowers are common. The fascicles on a plant that produces fruits annually are usually 1- to 4-flowered. Basically each unit of a female fascicle represents a reduced cyme with two sub-basal bracts indicating the position of the absent flowers (fig. 2 b,c).

The flowers of yaupon are 4-merous. Each flower has a green calyx with 4 small lobes and a white rotate corolla with a short tube and 4 oblong lobes rounded at the apex (fig. 1 f,g). The male flower has 4 stamens, each with a large oblong anther on a filament broadened at the base. The filaments are inserted at the throat of the short corolla tube and alternate with the lobes (fig. 1f). The ovary of a male flower is rudimentary and pulvinate-conic.

The stamens of a female flower are sterile with the filaments twice as long as the small ovate anthers (fig. 2 b,c). The pistil is large, ovoid, and terminated with a 4-lobed sessile stigma. The ovary has 4 locules, each containing one hanging ovule.

The yaupon flowers in April and May. Pollination is effected by insects. After fertilization, the ovary develops into a fruit. The male plants never bear fruits.

Fruits. In his lectures to students, Professor M. L. Fernald, author of the eighth edition of *Gray's Manual of Botany*, often quoted the Book of Matthew, saying "By their fruits ye shall know them" to emphasize the importance of fruit characters in the identification of species. It is especially so with the species of *Ilex*. The color, size, shape, the persistent calyx at the base, the discoid stigma at the apex, and the length of the fruiting stalk are important features for distinguishing hollies.

A mature fruit of yaupon is red, globose, 5–6 mm. in diame-

Figure 2. The female flowers, fruit, and seed of *Ilex vomitoria*. **a.** A female inflorescence showing an axillary fascicle with 7 flowers and a sterile central portion with scales, each flower representing a reduced cyme, the sub-basal bracts, indicating the positions of rudimentary flowers (Faxon 1888, × 4). **b.** The top view of a female flower showing 4 corolla lobes, 4 staminodes with ovate sterile anthers, and a large ovary with sessile stigma (Faxon 1888, × 9). **c.** The lateral view of the same flower showing the calyx, corolla, staminodes and ovary (× 9). **d, e.** The apical and basal views of a globose fruit showing the discoid stigma and the persistent calyx (Tarbox 22, × 4). **f.** The abaxial view of a pyrene showing the palmately striate and slightly sulcate surface (Godfrey and Tryon 652, × 9). **g.** The adaxial view of the same showing the reticulation of the vascular strands around the germination pore (× 9). **h.** The longitudinal section of a pyrene showing the woody endocarp (hatched), the germination pore (black), and the enclosed seed with a caruncle (dotted), thin funicle, very thin seed coat and copious endosperm (Godfrey and Tryon 652, × 9).

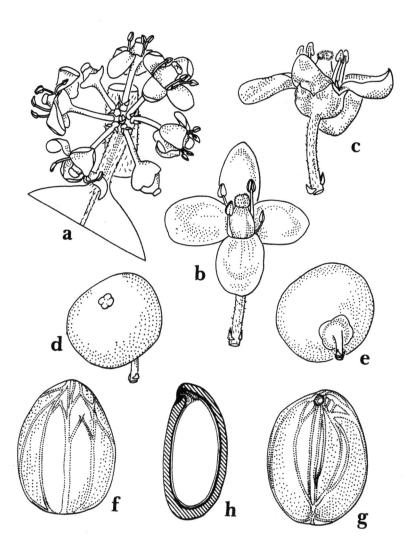

a

b

c

d

e

f

h

g

ter, with a discoid stigma at the apex and a persistent calyx at
the base (fig. 2 d,e). The stalk is 2 mm. long and bears sub-basal
bracts. A yellow-fruited form has occasionally been reported
from wild populations as well as from cultivation.

As the ovary develops into a mature fruit, its wall undergoes
differential changes, and the mature pericarp consists of three
distinctive layers. The outermost layer (exocarp) becomes
leathery and red (rarely yellow). The middle mass becomes
yellowish and fleshy (mesocarp). The innermost layer (endocarp) becomes lignified, forming a separated woody cover surrounding a single seed. The vascular strands cling to the
woody endocarp. Because the ovary of yaupon has 4 locules, a
fruit matures with 4 separated kernels (pyrenes).

A pyrene of holly is morphologically equivalent to the stone
of a peach or the pit of an olive. Yet it differs slightly from
both of these. An ovary of holly is compound like that of an
olive, but in holly the endocarps are separated while in the
olive they are fused. A peach stone is derived from a simple
carpel.

The size and shape of the pyrenes of yaupon are determined
by their position in the fruit as well as by the size of the fruit.
Because a pyrene occupies one-fourth of a small spherical fruit,
it is subtrigonous, with a slightly convex outer (abaxial) surface and two plane inner sides (adaxial surface). It is oblong-
ovoid in shape, 4 mm. long, and 3 mm. across. Both the adaxial
and abaxial surfaces are prominently palmate-striate. The
vascular strands are anastomosed toward the distal end. At the
distal end of the adaxial ridge there is a small depression, the
germination pore (fig. 2 g,h). A pyrene of yaupon is a lignified
closed case such that the enclosed seed has only one channel of
communication to the outside world, i.e., the germination pore.
The lignified wall does not degenerate readily. It never splits
except by the force of a germinating seed from the inside. It is
reinforced by the vascular strands on the outside and by fibrous
tissue on the inside.

Seeds. Most people take the pyrenes of a holly to be the seed, but in fact few people have ever seen a true seed of holly because it is completely hidden by the endocarp, which is very hard to open (fig. 2h). The seed of yaupon has the contour of the pyrene, and it fills the cavity of the pyrene. It has a very delicate thin hyaline seed coat, copious oily endosperm, and an underdeveloped embryo imperceptible even under a high-power dissecting microscope. Around the short funiculus (umbilical cord) there is a spongy tissue (caruncle), which plugs up the space inside the germination pore. The viability of the seed is protected from the chemical action within the alimentary canal of an animal (most likely a bird) ingesting it, or from the saline water of the coast, whichever the dispersal agent may be. Normally it takes one to three years for holly seeds to germinate. Perhaps the underdevelopment of the embryo is a contributing factor to the delayed germination of the seeds.

Special Garden Forms. In the late 1940s Professor Karl Sax, former director of the Arnold Arboretum, tried to combine the striking characters of the brilliant red fruit of the deciduous *Ilex verticillata* (L.) Gray and the dwarf habit and evergreen foliage of *Ilex glabra* (L.) Gray through hybridization. He wanted to produce an ornamental shrub for the northern gardens. Unfortunately the genetic makeups of these species are so different that no hybrid can be produced. For southern gardens, nature has produced *Ilex vomitoria* Ait. with all the desirable characteristics that Sax wanted to combine, and southern horticulturists and landscape gardeners are capitalizing on the unique merits of this species. They have selected outstanding forms, using them increasingly in foundation plantings, in hedges, for screens, and for other landscape purposes. In 1944 Tarbox reported a yellow fruit form, *I. vomitoria* 'Yawkeyi'. In 1960 Foret and Solymosy described a weeping form, *I. vomitoria* f. *pendula*. The 1970 issue of the *Handbook of Hollies* includes a picture of a variegated form, *I. vomitoria* 'Tricolor'. In the same handbook Eisenbeiss reported six more cultivars available in current nursery trade.

These are *I. vomitoria* 'DeWerth', 'Gray's Littleleaf', 'Gray's Weeping', 'Jewel', 'Pride of Texas' and 'Stokes Dwarf'. In 1971 Wyman, in the *Gardening Encyclopedia*, listed *I. vomitoria* 'Nana' as a dense growing dwarf form with small leaves and no fruit. *I. vomitoria* 'Otis Miley' is a yellow-fruited form with elliptic-oblong leaves 1.5–2.6 cm. long, 5–10 mm. wide, and obtuse at both ends. It is cultivated in Ida Cason Callaway garden at Pine Mountain, Georgia. On a specimen collected in January 1960 by Fred C. Galle, the origin of this form is given as Bogalusa, Louisiana.

NOMENCLATURE

The nomenclature of yaupon has been terribly confused, with over a dozen binary scientific names applied to the species by different authors. The nomenclature of plants is a dry and complicated subject. It entails many principles and procedural rules that may be boring to the nonspecialist reader. In tackling the major nomenclatural problems related to yaupon, in the pages that follow I have undertaken three tasks of increasing degrees of complexity. The reader may stop at the point at which his intellectual curiosity is satisfied. (1) For clarity in the communication of information, I ascertain the correct scientific name and consistently use one common name for the species which the southeastern Indians used in making black drink. (2) For assisting researchers in the collection of information from literature or from plant material in the field, I present a chronological list of botanical names and an alphabetic list of vernacular names taken from published records or specimens. (3) In order to explain some of the outstanding causes of confusion encountered in the application of scientific names related to the economic uses and ethnobotanical aspects of the species, I present a few case studies.

The correct scientific name of yaupon is *Ilex vomitoria* Ait. This name was first published in 1789 in the *Hortus Kewensis*. Aiton's material was cultivated in the Royal Botanic Gardens

at Kew outside London. For the native country of the species
Aiton gave "West Florida."

According to Aiton the species was introduced to London in
1700. Leonard Plukenet, a doctor in Westminster, first cultivated it. In that year Plukenet published a description of it
under the phrase-name, *Cassine vera Floridanorum*. This descriptive name was used in gardens around London, and it was
the name used in most of the botanical literature of the first
half of the eighteenth century. Mark Catesby adopted this
name in his *Natural History of Carolina, Florida and the Bahama Islands*, but with a slight change of spelling, making it
Cassena vera Floridanorum. Aiton cited both Plukenet and
Catesby as references and gave the current English names as
South-Sea Tea and Ever-green Cassine.

According to Miller (1754), *Cassine vera Floridanorum*
soared to popularity in European gardens as an ornamental
plant because its bright red fruits "intermixed with the green
Leaves, make a fine Appearance . . . [in] . . . most Part of the
Winter, . . . [but] the severe Frost in the Year 1740 . . . destroyed all the Plants in the Garden near London." These
plants were propagated from seeds obtained in Carolina.

A chronological list of synonyms of *Ilex vomitoria* Ait. follows.

> 1753. *Ilex cassine* L. var. b.
>
> 1753. *Cassine peragua* L., *pro parte*.
>
> 1762. *Prinos glaber* L., *pro parte*.
>
> 1768. *Cassine paragua* Miller, *sphalm*.
>
> 1782. *Cassine caroliniana* Lamarck.
>
> 1788. *Ilex cassine* Walter, *non Linnaeus*.
>
> 1791. *Ilex floridana* Lamarck.
>
> 1791. *Cassine yapon* Bartram, *nom. nud*.
>
> 1803. *Ilex cassena* Michaux.
>
> 1812. *Ilex religiosa* Barton.
>
> 1830. *Hierophyllus cassine* Rafinesque.
>
> 1838. *Ageria cassena* Rafinesque.
>
> 1889. *Ilex peragua* (L.) Trelease.
>
> 1891. *Ilex caroliniana* (Lam.) Loesener.
>
> 1946. *Cassine vomitoria* Swanton, *nom. nud*.

The name of a species is a binary combination consisting of the name of the genus followed by a single specific epithet. The phrase-names of yaupon used in early botanical literature have no standing in modern nomenclature. The correct name for yaupon is *Ilex vomitoria* Ait., and this is the accepted name in all modern floras, manuals, horticultural encyclopedias, dictionaries of gardening, and handbooks of hollies.

An alphabetic list of vernacular names of *Ilex vomitoria* Ait. follows.

American tea plant	Cassine	Evergreen cassine
Apalachine	Cassines	South-Sea tea
Casino-berry	Cassio-berry	Tree cassena
Cassena	Christmas-berry tree	Yapon
Cassena tree	Coon berry	Yaupon
Cassiana	Emetic holly	Yopon
Cassina	Evergreen cassena	Youpon

The confusion in the application of scientific names to yaupon began in the second half of the eighteenth century and increased in the botanical literature of the nineteenth century. By the early twentieth century it subsided, for by that time most authors had adopted *Ilex vomitoria* as the correct name of yaupon. The initiation, growth, and subsidence of the nomenclatural confusion of *I. vomitoria* followed a typical course in the stream of botanical history. Each instance that contributed to this confusion can be regarded as a specific historical juncture. When each instance of confusion is analyzed and its position in the stream of history isolated, its effect on obscuring a stable system of nomenclature can be minimized. The cases I have selected for discussion are Carl Linnaeus, Thomas Walter, Asa Gray, J.B.A.P.M. de Lamarck, André Michaux, Benjamin Smith Barton, Theodor Loesener, and Constantine Samuel Rafinesque. In reviewing these cases we can better appreciate the accomplishments and the difficulties of the pioneer botanists who had to work in isolation without sufficient material, without definite criteria for identification of species, and without established rules of nomenclature. These difficulties, plus the eccentric personalities of some of these pioneer botanists, contributed to the nomenclatural confusion of yaupon.

The publication date of Carl Linnaeus's *Species Plantarum* (1753) is accepted internationally as the starting point of the binomial nomenclatural system for flowering plants. When Linnaeus prepared this work he examined a limited number of specimens and drew on the work of many authors. In regard to American holly, which he placed in the genus *Ilex*, he had two herbarium specimens and nine references. He recognized one of the specimens as the living plant growing in the garden of George Clifford of Holland, where he had spent three years as physician and as superintendent of the garden. He labeled this specimen *Ilex cassine*. Linnaeus could not identify the other specimen, and he put "Ilex" on this herbarium sheet. This specimen was evidently yaupon, and it is material proof that Linnaeus did not have a clear conception of the plant described by Plukenet and Catesby as *Cassine vera floridanorum*, otherwise he would have given it this designation.

In compiling his *Species Plantarum* Linnaeus cited several references which he considered applicable to *Ilex cassine* and divided them into two categories, one for the species and the other for variety *b*. For the species *Ilex cassine*, Linnaeus cited as references "*Hort, clif. 40, Catesb. car. I. p. 31. t. 31.*" To this species he annexed variety *b*, citing as references "Cassine vera floridanorum . . . *Pluk. mant. 40, Catesb. car. 2 p. 57. t. 57.*" Linnaeus's inclusion of two elements in *Ilex cassine* is the source of all subsequent nomenclatural confusion.

Thomas Walter was an early settler in South Carolina. On his plantation by the edge of the Santee River Swamp, he established a garden around his house, where he cultivated native as well as introduced species. The only contact he had with the outside world was an itinerant seedsman from London, John Fraser. Stimulated by his keen interest in the native plants, Walter prepared a manuscript written in Latin, entitled *Flora Caroliniana*. It contains a description of plants collected

within a radius of 50 miles of his home. After Walter's death
John Fraser brought this manuscript to London and published
it in 1788. In this work Walter described two new species of
Ilex, naming them *I. cassine* Walter and *I. Dahoon* Walter. He
characterized the former species as having ovate leaves, obtuse
at the ends and serrate along the margin, and the second one
as having lanceolate-elliptic leaves, subentire along the margin.
As Walter's *I. cassine* refers to plants different from *I. cassine*
L., it becomes a later homonym and has no legal standing in
botanical usage. References to *I. cassine* Walter in any botanical literature should be treated as statements for *I. vomitoria*
Ait.

   Asa Gray's *Manual of Botany of the Northern United States*
is practically the botanical bible for students of eastern American botany, and it is an important reference work in the northern temperate regions of other parts of the world. In the
various editions of the *Manual,* Gray misinterpreted Linnaeus's
Ilex cassine and applied it to yaupon. This unfortunate misinterpretation first appeared in the revised edition of the
Manual published in 1857, and it persisted in succeeding editions. The mistake was not corrected until 1908, when B. L.
Robinson and M. L. Fernald published the seventh edition of
the *Manual.*

   Gray's misinterpretation of the Linnaean species was further
compounded through the work of his followers, especially Alvin Wentworth Chapman's work on the southern flora and
Edwin M. Hale's work on yaupon. Alvin Wentworth Chapman
was born and educated in Massachusetts. He went to Georgia
for a medical education and later practiced surgery in Florida.
He was interested in the study of the plants of the South. He
sent specimens to Asa Gray for identification. In 1860 Chapman published *Flora of the Southern United States,* which
includes a description of *Ilex cassine* (yaupon). Edwin M. Hale
was a physician who practiced in Chicago. In 1891 he published a review of scattered information on yaupon, including
a very good summary of its etymology, chemistry, history, dis-

tribution (with a map), and uses. This has been a much quoted reference on yaupon. Unfortunately the illustration is botanically inaccurate and the nomenclature was adopted from the floras and manuals of the time. He was personally acquainted with Chapman. The *Ilex cassine* in Hale's article should be referred to as *I. vomitoria* Ait.

In the first two decades of the twentieth century, American botanists adopted the practice of identifying species by comparing their specimens with the nomenclatural types, that is, with the specimens used by the authors who named and described the species. Consequently they found that the type of *Ilex cassine* L. in the Linnaean herbarium refers not to yaupon but to the dahoon holly of the eastern United States. The correct name for yaupon is *I. vomitoria* Ait.

Jean Baptiste Antoine Pierre Monnet, Chevalier de Lamarck, was a leading French botanist in the late eighteenth century. He misunderstood Miller's account of *Cassine corymbosa*, mistaking it for "Cassine de la Caroline." In 1782 he proposed the name *Cassine caroliniana* for it. This specific epithet was adopted by Theodor Loesener as the basinym of *Ilex caroliniana* (Lam.) Loes. It is by this name that yaupon appears in Loesener's *Monographia Aquifoliacearum*, a classical reference work on the holly family. Lamarck's name appeared in print several years earlier than that of Aiton's, but it cannot be applied to yaupon because it involves two elements and it refers primarily to *Viburnum corymbosum* (Miller) Rehder. Loesener did not realize that when he made the combination *Ilex caroliniana* (Lam.) Loes., the epithet was antedated by *Ilex caroliniana* (Walter) Trelease, a name referring to a completely different species of *Ilex*. Obviously Loesener's Lamarckian epithet, *Ilex caroliniana* (Lam.) Loes., is illegitimate, and it cannot be taken as the correct name for yaupon.

In regard to the names proposed by André Michaux and Benjamin Smith Barton, I can see no justification other than the assertion of the freedom of choice in the selection of names. André Michaux made botanical explorations for twelve years in the United States for the French government. In his *Flora Boreali-americana* he listed *Ilex cassine* Walt. and *Cassena vera* Catesby. Instead of using the name that had already been placed in the genus *Ilex* by Walter, he chose Catesby's spelling, thus creating *Ilex cassena* Michx. This spelling was also adopted by Stephen Elliott in his *A Sketch of Botany of South-Carolina and Georgia* (1824).

Benjamin Smith Barton in his *Flora Virginica* listed all the references of Aiton, Miller, Plukenet, Catesby, and Michaux. Instead of adopting one of the names of these authors, as he had in his earlier publications, where he used *Ilex vomitoria* Ait. for yaupon, he proposed a new name here, *Ilex religiosa* Barton. Perhaps, after observing the rituals in which the southeastern Indians drank black drink, he thought his choice would be a more appropriate epithet to indicate the ethnobotanical significance of the plant. The following quotation may help to explain what was in his mind. "Comparing this [Indian tea] tradition with that of the Chinese . . . [who first discovered tea], . . . it is impossible not to perceive, that both of the traditions have a common origin: and the natural and irresistible inference is, that some of our Indians have sprung from China." Whatever their motivations were, Michaux and Barton merely added to a long list of synonyms for *Ilex vomitoria* Ait.

In the space of eight years, Constantine Samuel Rafinesque managed to place the species that we call *Ilex vomitoria* Ait. into two different genera, calling them *Hierophyllus cassine* Raf. and *Ageria cassena* Raf. It happened in the following manner. In 1830 in a discussion of the history of *Ilex opaca* Ait., Rafinesque boldly announced, "The Genus *Ilex* of Linnaeus contains many heterogeneous species. . . . As early as 1817 I separated [one group] . . . calling it Nemopanthus. . . . The *Ilex Cassine* or *Vomitoria* must form a particular genus. . . . I propose to call it Hierophyllus Cassine."

In 1838 he redefined *Ageria* Adanson and grouped the New World species of *Ilex* into three subgenera under the genus *Ageria*. He proposed *Ageria cassena* to replace *I. vomitoria*

Ait. and designated it to be the type species of *Ageria* subgenus *Dahunia* Raf. Rafinesque is notorious in botanical literature. Most botanists consider him to be an utterly irresponsible super-erratic person. Professor Elmer Drew Merrill, former director of the Arnold Arboretum, commended him as having a brilliant intellect but an eccentric character. He said that Rafinesque was "versatile, positive, . . . with a phenomenal memory, an unusually wide knowledge of language, uncontrolled and incontrollable, . . . convinced that his mission was to correct the errors of all of his contemporaries and predecessors in the wide realm of biology." All these comments apply to Rafinesque in his creation of the synonyms for *Ilex vomitoria* Ait.

The names proposed after 1789 and those marked *nomen nudum* are inconsequential in the nomenclature of yaupon because as superfluous names they have no standing in botanical nomenclature.

A name is only a device used to communicate information. When there are two or more names for a single thing, or one name for two or more things, confusion is inevitable. Both of these sources of confusion are found in the nomenclature of yaupon. *Ilex vomitoria* Ait. (1789) is ascertained to be the correct scientific name for yaupon. In order to avoid future confusion, it is suggested that *yaupon* be used as the standard common name for *I. vomitoria* Ait.

We have seen that in the botanical history of the eastern United States, the homeland of yaupon, from the middle of the nineteenth century until the early portion of the twentieth century, authors of the major floras of the area misinterpreted *Ilex cassine* L. (a name typified by a specimen of dahoon holly) and applied it to yaupon. Reports on the economic and medicinal uses and the chemical composition of yaupon dating from the same period also use *Ilex cassine* for yaupon. Researchers using such references are reminded of the nomenclatural confusion and are advised to use *I. vomitoria* Ait. for yaupon and to reserve *I. cassine* L. for dahoon holly, which is a very different species.[1]

Figure 3. *Ilex cassine.* **a.** The habit sketch of a fruiting specimen showing the branching system with shoots developing from both the terminal and the lateral buds, bearing fruits below and leaves above (Texas, Thorne 7341, × 1/3). **b.** A male inflorescence showing a stalked trichotomously branched cluster axillary to a reduced leaf (Florida, Cooley and Eaton 6624, × 2). **c.** A female inflorescence showing a 3-flowered loose cluster axillary to a leaf. Note the central flower opens first and the lateral ones follow (Florida, Cooley et al. 6182, × 2).

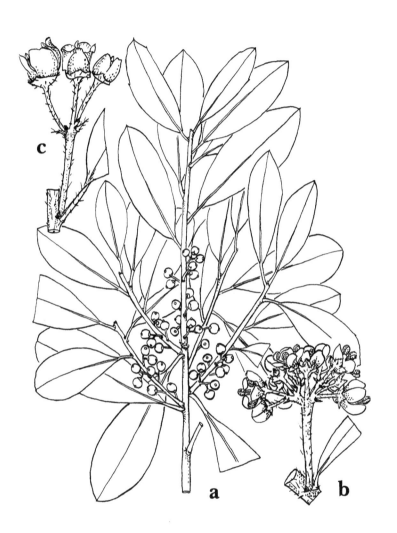

c

a

b

RELATED SPECIES

Modern systematists have developed many devices for obtaining internal as well as external evidences for assessing relationships among species. These devices require equipment, time, care, and patience. Very few of them have as yet been applied to the study of the genus *Ilex*. Data pertinent to the cytology, anatomy, pollen morphology, and chemistry of *I. vomitoria* are not yet available. Hence the determination of relationships must be made primarily on the basis of morphological distinctness with some support from geographical distribution and the genetic record. These evidences testify that in the holly family the position of *I. vomitoria* is considerably isolated. It has no closely related species within the United States. Its few immediate relatives occur in the West Indies. Some distant relatives occur in Mexico, Honduras, and eastern Asia. Numerous remotely related species occur in the tropical regions of both hemispheres.

In the 1970 edition of the *Handbook of Hollies,* twenty-one species of *Ilex* native to the United States are recognized. Among its compatriots, *I. vomitoria* has no close relatives. It is the only species of the United States that has evergreen crenulate-serrate small leaves, fasciculate inflorescences, and red fruits each with four separate woody pyrenes. These morphological characteristics are manifestations of genetic distinctions. The results of the hybridizations performed by William Kosar in the United States National Arboretum have proved the incompatibility of *I. vomitoria* with its compatriots. Up to the time when I visited the National Arboretum in August 1963, of his numerous crosses Kosar had been able to produce only F_1 hybrids of *I. vomitoria* with two cultivars of Chinese species, that is, *Ilex* 'Cornuta-pernyi' and *Ilex* 'Nellie', a garden selection of *I. cornuta* Lindl.

In order to assess the relationships between *I. vomitoria* and other species of *Ilex,* I have reexamined all the specimens in Harvard University Herbaria under strong illumination with a dissecting microscope. I found three montane species from the West Indies which share the fundamental morphological distinctions of *I. vomitoria*. These are *I. ligustrina* Jacq. of Cuba, and two species from the Dominican Republic, *I. barahonica* Loes. and *I. fuertesiana* (Loes.) Loes. Of these three species, *I. fuertesiana* resembles *I. vomitoria* most closely. In the shape and size of the leaves they are hardly distinguishable. *Ilex fuertesiana* occurs in remnants of primitive cloud forests at altitudes of 1800–2000 m. *Ilex barahonica* occurs in shady forests at altitudes of 400–1300 m. at Monteada Nueva Caña Brava, Barahona. Compared to *I. vomitoria* its leaves are thin and proportionally wider and with inconspicuous marginal teeth. *Ilex ligustrina* has larger and thinner leaves with cuneate base and round apex. It occurs in woods at altitudes of 500 m.

Ilex chiapensis (Sharp) S. Y. Hu is a closely related species of the subtropical forests in the moist ravines of Chiapas, Hidalgo, and Veracruz in Mexico.[2] Morphologically it has a distinctive long and loose indumentum on the shoots and leaves. The ovate or oblong thin leaves with evident lateral veins and rather sharp teeth resemble those of *I. fuertesiana* of the Hispaniola in size, shape, texture, and dentation. The three Caribbean species and the two mainland species form the series Vomitoriae.

In the forests of Mexico and Honduras there are three species that are distantly related to *I. vomitoria*. These are *I. discolor* Hemsl. and *I. californica* Brandegee of Mexico, and *I. hondurensis* Standley of Honduras. These species are widely separated. They share with *I. vomitoria* the characters of fasciculate inflorescences, spherical red fruits on short pedicels, and palmately striate-sulcate woody pyrenes. Their evergreen crenulate-serrate leaves are much larger than those of *I. vomitoria*. All three species are trees 7–9 m. high. *Ilex discolor* occurs in oak forests on steep rugged limestone slopes at altitudes of 1400–1600 m. near Ciudad del Maiz in San Luis Potosi. *Ilex hondurensis* occurs in pine-oak woods along streams in ravines at altitudes about 1350 m. in Situatepeque, Honduras.

Ilex californica occurs on Sierra de la Laguna of Baja California.

In dealing with the relationships of species in the genus *Ilex,* one encounters the interesting phenomenon of bicentric distribution of closely related Old World and New World species. The counterpart of the central American arborescent species is found in China and Japan. For example, it would be difficult for even a specialist to distinguish the leafless flowering or fruiting branches of *I. discolor* and *I. hondurensis* from that of *I. cinerea* Champ. ex Benth., a species growing in the forest of steep windy slopes of Hongkong Peak. They all belong to series Cinereae.

The remotely related species of *I. vomitoria* belong to the series Repandae. This series contains over thirty species distributed in the tropics and subtropics of both hemispheres. In the New World the species are widely separated. There is one species on the Pacific coast of Baja California, *I. socorroensis* Brandegee from Socorro Island. On the Atlantic side there are *I. repanda* Griseb. from Cuba and the Bahamas, and *I. nitida* (Vahl) Maxim. from Jamaica and Puerto Rico. On the mainland there are *I. tolucana* Hemsl. from Nuevo Leon of northeastern Mexico, *I. lamprophylla* Standley from the dense wet forest of Costa Rica, and *I. davidsoniae* Standley from the rain forest in Panama. In South America there is *I. guayusa* Loes. of Ecuador and northern Peru, which recently has been obtained as an archaeological specimen from a 1500-year-old tomb in Bolivia. Farther south, in southeastern Brazil and adjacent Argentina and Paraguay, there is *I. paraguariensis* St. Hil. It is worth noting that *I. guayusa* and *I. paraguariensis* are morphologically very different from all the remaining South American species of *Ilex,* and that they are geographically and ecologically associated with man. There seems to be room for questioning whether their distributions represent the natural extension of the range of series Repandae to South America. Their distributions could have been prehistoric man-made extensions produced by the aboriginal peoples of South America, who used them in religious ceremonies, for tea, and for snuff.

The evolutionary lines of the genus *Ilex* almost always exhibit obvious reductional changes from large to small leaves and from loose to compact inflorescences. Both of these reductional changes are present in most groups of South American *Ilex,* but neither is present in the Repandae-Cinereae-Vomitoriae line in that continent.

In the Old World the series Repandae contains about twenty species occurring from Assam of northeastern India (*I. odorata* Ham. ex D. Don) eastward through China (*I. intermedia* Loes.) and Indochina (*I. tonkiniana* Loes.), Hongkong (*I. ficoidea* Hemsl.), Taiwan (*I. formosana* Maxim.), Okinawa (*I. liukiuensis* Loes.), and Japan (*I. buergeri* Miq.), and thence southward to Malaysia and Indonesia (*I. glomerata* King).

From the facts summarized above, the following inferences may be made.

1. It is clear that *I. vomitoria* is of tropical origin. All its remote relatives are trees occurring in the wet forests in the tropics of both hemispheres. Its distant relatives are trees of mixed forests of higher altitude in the tropics and subtropics of both the Old and the New Worlds. Its closely related species are specialized forms occurring in cloud forests in the Caribbean.

2. All the closely related species of *I. vomitoria* are members of cloud forests. From the ecological background of its relatives, the montane population of *I. vomitoria* of the Ouachita Mountain area in western Arkansas and eastern Oklahoma may be interpreted as the original stock of the species. The populations of the coastal plains are derived ecological forms adapted for the harsh life of semi-xeric conditions of the seashore, hammocks, and bluffs.

3. The distributions of the closely, distantly, and remotely related species of *I. vomitoria* indicate an evolutionary history through time and space. During the Tertiary period, when there were more floristic exchanges between land masses of the earth, more species of *Ilex* existed in the eastern United States than exist there today. Paleobotanical records indicate this to be true. Alfred Traverse's pollen analysis of the Bran-

don lignite of Vermont reveals six species of *Ilex* in the Oligocene deposit. In the same area today there is only one deciduous species, *I. verticillata* (L.) Gray. Traverse's most striking finding was the pollen grain of one species which he could not distinguish from that of *I. chinensis* Sims, now growing in the warm parts of China and Japan. Traverse named this fossil specimen *I. chinensis* in his report and described all the others as new to science.

The relationship of *I. vomitoria* with Asiatic species is proved by Kosar's hybridization work. This relationship was established in geological time, and *I. vomitoria* is a relict species.

4. According to my studies in the evolution and distribution of the species in the genus *Ilex*, the basic characteristics of *I. vomitoria* and its related species place them in the advanced group of the genus. In *Ilex* the tendency of evolutionary changes from conditions of generalization to specialization is the reduction in number of flowers and floral parts and the reduction in size of the vegetative organs. The small leaves and compact inflorescences of the series Vomitoriae indicate an advanced stage of evolutionary specialization. Hence *Ilex vomitoria* is a highly specialized advanced species in the genus *Ilex*.

SPECIES OF ILEX USED FOR TEA

For those who are interested in the economic importance and the ethnobotanical significance of *I. vomitoria,* several questions naturally arise: Is *I. vomitoria* related to *I. paraguariensis* since they both contain caffeine? Are other species of *Ilex* used for tea, and if so, do they contain caffeine? In an article dealing with *I. guayusa*, Professor R. E. Schultes reviewed the literature on twenty-five species of *Ilex* used for tea. These are listed alphabetically below. All the species except those with remarks in parentheses are from South America.

> *Ilex affinis* Gardn.
> *Ilex amara* (Vell.) Loes.

Ilex chamaedryfolia Reiss. ex Mart.
Ilex cognata Reiss. ex Mart.
Ilex congonhina Loes.
Ilex conocarpa Reiss. ex Mart.
Ilex cuiabensis Reiss. ex Mart.
Ilex diuretica Mart.
Ilex dumosa Reiss. ex Mart.
Ilex fertilis Reiss. ex Mart.
Ilex glabra (L.) A. Gray (eastern USA)
Ilex glaziouviana Loes.
Ilex guayusa Loes.
Ilex opaca Ait. (*I. Quercifolia* Meerbg., eastern USA)
Ilex paltorioides Reiss. ex Mart.
Ilex paraguariensis St. Hil.
Ilex pseudobuxus Reiss. ex Mart.
Ilex pseudothea Reiss. ex Mart.
Ilex symplociformis Reiss. ex Mart.
Ilex tarapotina Loes.
Ilex theezans Mart.
Ilex verticillata (L.) A. Gray (eastern USA)
Ilex vitis-idaea Loes.
Ilex vomitoria Ait. (southeastern USA)
Ilex yunnanensis Franch. var. *eciliata* S. Y. Hu
   (Sino-Tibetan border)

Ilex vomitoria is distantly related to *I. guayusa* and *I. paraguariensis* but unrelated to the rest of the species listed above. Regarding the caffeine content, no data are available for the species other than *I. vomitoria, I. guayusa,* and *I. paraguariensis.* All three species contain caffeine, and they have been used for tea by the native peoples of North and South America since prehistoric times.

SUMMARY

This article deals with the distinctive characters, the correct name, and the affinity of a species of plant which is commonly called yaupon. The correct scientific name of the species is *Ilex vomitoria* Ait.

The species is an evergreen shrub with small oblong or elliptic-ovate leaves which are crenulate-serrate along the margin and obtuse or rounded at both ends. The flowers are small, white, unisexual, borne in axils of leaves on the second year's or rarely on older growth, and 4-merous. The fruits are red, spherical, on short pedicels, and contain 4 separate woody pyrenes. The pyrene is palmately striate-sulcate and with some reticulation surrounding the germination pore.

The center of morphological diversity of the species is the Gulf Coast, especially on the Florida side, and particularly in the area between longitudes 82°30′–85°W and latitudes 28°–30°30′N. The populations on the periphery of the specific range are more uniform in the size and shape of the leaves.

Species sharing the basic morphological characters of *I. vomitoria* are considered to be closely related. They occur in the cloud forest of the West Indies. Species with similar flowering and fruiting characters but with larger leaves are considered to be distant relatives of *I. vomitoria*.

They occur in the oak-pine forests of Mexico and Honduras, and also in Hongkong and other regions of southeastern Asia. Species with similar pyrene character but with looser flowering and fruiting clusters and larger leaves prominently crenate or serrate are considered remote relatives of *I. vomitoria*. There are over thirty species of them in the tropical wet forests of both hemispheres.

From the distribution of the related species of *I. vomitoria* it is concluded that yaupon had a tropical origin and that it is an ancient montane species. The population of the Ouachita Mountain area is a relict, and those of the coastal plains are derived forms specialized for the semi-xeric condition of the sand dunes of beaches, hammocks, and bluffs.

Available records indicate that twenty-five species of *Ilex* are used for tea by ethnic groups in South America, North America, and the Sino-Tibetan mountainous area. The caffeine content of three of the species, *I. vomitoria*, *I. paraguariensis*, and *I. guayusa*, has been confirmed.

NOTES

1. There should be no confusion in the application of the scientific names of the two native American hollies, *Ilex vomitoria* Ait. for yaupon and *I. cassine* L. for dahoon. The following comparison of the important characteristics of the species may help the reader to distinguish them and to apply the correct names.

Both yaupon and dahoon have evergreen foliage and red fruit. Their obvious differences are in their habit and in the size and margin of their leaves. In general, yaupons are shrubs with small leaves toothed along the margin (fig. 1a), while dahoons are trees with large entire leaves (fig. 3a). These characters are subjected to the influence of environmental factors. The primary and more constant distinctions of the species lie in the nature of their buds, the architecture of their branching systems, and the arrangement of their flowers into inflorescences. The buds of yaupon are specialized in structure and function. The flower buds unfold into the male or the female fascicles (figs. 1e, 2a), and the vegetative buds develop into leafy shoots (fig. 1a) under normal conditions. In dahoon the buds are mixed, and when a bud unfolds, it at first gives rise to flowers and then continues to develop into a leafy shoot (fig. 3a). This generalized function of the buds in dahoon leads to its characteristic branching system. In dahoon every twig of a mature normal plant can bear both flowers and leaves, and in any given year's growth of a female plant it has fruit below the leaves. In yaupon the flowers are in fascicles, each consisting of many 1–3-flowered units in the male plant (fig. 1e), or 1-flowered units in the female plant (fig. 2a). In dahoon the flowers are not in fascicles, but they are arranged in loose, stalked clusters in the axils of normal or reduced leaves, or scales, scattered on the lower portion of the current year's growth. The male flower-cluster consists of 12 to 25 flowers trichotomously branched (fig. 3b), and the female flower-cluster contains 3 or rarely up to 5 flowers (fig. 2c). Normally some of the female flowers drop off, and 1, 2 or 3 of them develop into fruits (fig. 3a). In dahoon (*I. cassine* L.) wherever there are more fruits growing together than one, they share a common stalk. This condition does not occur in yaupon (*I. vomitoria* Ait.). The fruits of yaupon are attached to the stem individually (fig. 1a); those of dahoon may join the stem in clusters of two or three (fig. 3a).

2. This species was first discovered in 1945 by Professor Aaron J. Sharp of the University of Tennessee and his Mexican colleague Ffraín Herándex Xolocotzi in several localities of Chiapas. In 1950 it was named and described as *I. vomitoria* Ait. var. *chiapensis* Sharp. In 1949 H. E. Moore collected it on slopes with pine-oak and moss-

covered beech-magnolia woods in a ravine near Zacualtipan, Hidalgo. Wayne E. Manning in 1953 and A. Gomez Pompa in 1962 collected it in Vera Cruz. Its relationship with the American species (*I. vomitoria*), the Caribbean species (*I. barahonica, I. fuertesiana, I. ligustrina*) and with other Mexican species (*I. discolor, I. californica*, etc.) forms a reticulate complex. It cannot be treated as a variety of any of these species, hence it is raised to specific rank. *Ilex chiapensis* (Sharp) S. Y. Hu, stat. nov. (Basinym: *I. vomitoria* Ait. var. *chiapensis* Sharp in Contr. Bot. Lab. Univ. Tenn., n.s. 118. 1950.)

LITERATURE CITED

Aiton, W. 1789. *Hortus Kewensis*. London: George Nicol.

Bartram, W. 1791. *Travels through North and South Carolina*. Philadelphia: James and Johnson.

Barton, B. S. 1801–1804. *Collection for an Essay towards a Materia Medica*. Philadelphia: Edward Earle.

———. 1802. *Elements of Botany*. Philadelphia: University of Pennsylvania.

———. 1812. *Flora Virginica*. Philadelphia: Heartt.

Catesby, M. 1754. *The Natural History of Carolina, Florida and the Bahama Islands*. London: Benjamin White.

Chapman, A. W. 1860. *Flora of the Southern United States*. New York: Ivison, Phinney and Co.

Eisenbeiss, G. S., 1970. Hollies currently available in the trade. *Am. Hort. Mag.* 49:324 (*Handbook of Hollies*, ed. D. E. Hansell).

Elliott, S. 1821–24. *A Sketch of the Botany of South Carolina and Georgia*. Charleston: Schenck.

Fernald, M. L., and Kinsey, A. C. 1943. *Edible Wild Plants of Eastern North America*. Cornwall-on-Hudson, N.Y.: Idlewood Press.

———. 1950. *Gray's Manual of Botany*. 8th ed. New York: American Book Co.

Foret, J. A., and Solymosy, S. L. 1960. A new variant of Ilex vomitoria. *Baileya* 8:83.

Gray, A. 1857. *Manual of Botany of the Northern United States*. Rev. ed. New York: Putnam.

Hale, E. M. 1891. Ilex cassine, the aboriginal North American tea. *U.S.D.A. Div. Bot. Bull.* no. 14, pp. 7–22. Washington: Gov. Print. Office.

Hu, S. Y. 1949–50. The genus Ilex in China. *J. Arn. Arb.* 30: 233–44, 348–87; 31: 39–80, 214–63.

———. 1964. Fruit Characters in Holly. *Am. Hort. Mag.* 43: 21–32.

———. 1967. The evolution and distribution of the species of Aquifoliaceae in the Pacific Area. *J. Jap. Bot.* 42: 13–47, 49–59.

Jacquin, N. J. 1790. *Collectanea ad botanicam, chemiam, et historiam naturalem spectantia.* Vienna: Officina Wappleriana.

———. 1781–93. *Icones plantarum rariorum.* 3 vols. Vienna: Wappler.

Lamarck, J.B.A.P.M. de. 1785. *Encyclopédie méthodique.* Paris: Pankoucke.

Hansell, D. E., ed. 1970. Handbook of Hollies. *Am. Hort. Mag.* 49: 150–331.

Linnaeus, C. 1753. *Species plantarum.* Stockholm: Laurentii Salvii.

Loesener, T. 1901. Monographia Aquifoliacearum. *Nova Acta Abh. Kais. Leop.-Carol. Akad. Nat.* 78: 1–589.

Merrill, E. D. 1949. *Index rafinesquianus.* Baltimore: Lord Baltimore Press.

Michaux, A. 1803. *Flora boreali-americana.* Paris: Levroult.

Miller, P. 1754. *The Gardeners Dictionary.* London: Rivington.

Patiño, V. M. 1968. Guayusa, a neglected stimulant from the eastern Andean foothills. *Econ. Bot.* 22: 311–16.

Plukenet, L. 1700. *Almagesti botanici mantissa.* London: Private.

Rafinesque, C. S. 1830. *Medical Flora (Manual of the Medical Botany of the United States of North America).* Philadelphia: Atkinson and Alexander.

———. 1838. *Sylva telluriana mantissa synoptica.* Philadelphia: Private.

Rehder, A. 1922. New species, varieties and combinations from the herbarium and the collections of the Arnold Arboretum. *J. Arn. Arb.* 3: 212–14.

Robinson, B. L., and Fernald, M. L. 1908. *Gray's Manual of Botany.* 7th ed. New York: American Book Co.

Sharp, A. J. 1950. A new variety of Ilex vomitoria from southern Mexico. *Bot. Mus. Leafl. Harvard Univ.* 14: 107–8.

Schultes, R. E. 1950. The correct name of the yaupon. *Bot. Mus. Leafl. Harvard Univ.* 14: 97–105.

———. 1972. Ilex guayusa from 500 A.D. to the present. In S. H. Wassen, A medicine-man's implements and plants in a Tiahuanacoid tomb in highland Bolivia. *Etnol. Stud. Goteborg.* 32: 115–38.

Traverse, A. 1956. Pollen analysis of the Brandon lignite of Vermont. *Report. Investig. U.S. Dept. Interior Bur. Mines.* 5151: 1–107.

Trelease, W. 1889. Revision of North American Ilicineae and Celastraceae. *Trans. St. Louis Acad. Sci.* 5: 343–57.

Walter, T. 1788. *Flora caroliniana.* London: J. Wenman.

Wyman, D. 1971. *Gardening Encyclopedia.* New York: Macmillan Co.

The Beloved Tree:
Ilex vomitoria among the Indians of
the Southeast and Adjacent Regions

William L. Merrill

Ilex vomitoria grows along the Atlantic and Gulf coasts from southern Virginia, across central Florida, to southern Texas, spreading inland onto the expansive coastal plains of the Gulf States, the southeastern corner of Oklahoma, and the southwestern portions of Arkansas (see map 1). Apparently most if not all the Indian groups who lived where this plant is native employed black drink for one purpose or another. In addition, several Indian groups located beyond the natural range of *Ilex vomitoria* secured their supplies through trade or by planting groves of the shrub adjacent to their towns.

The purpose of this chapter is to provide a general descriptive overview of the use of black drink in aboriginal North America. The information presented here has been gleaned from the major early reports and more recent ethnographies that deal with the Indian groups who traditionally inhabited the Southeast and its northern and western peripheries. Unfortunately the ethnographic coverage of many of these Indian

This research was begun in 1972 under the auspices of the Department of Anthropology of the Smithsonian Institution with financial support provided by the National Science Foundation. I gratefully acknowledge the assistance of these institutions. I also would like to express my appreciation to Jo Ann Moore for preparing the maps that appear here and to Diane Della-Loggia, Mildred M. Wedel, Maurice L. Zigmond, Susan K. Brown, Rosemary M. DeRosa, Samuel Stanley, and the staff of the Center for the Study of Man, Smithsonian Institution, for their assistance in this project. Finally, I am especially indebted to William C. Sturtevant for his inspiration, guidance, and friendship during the completion of this project.

groups is spotty, making it difficult to determine with any degree of certainty the exact limits of the distribution of the use of black drink in native North America. Furthermore, it is close to impossible in the case of most groups to gain more than a superficial understanding of the nature of the contexts within which they consumed black drink or of the beliefs that they associated with it. Nonetheless, the information I presently have at hand belies the common assumption that the use of black drink was restricted to and universal among the Indian groups who resided in the southeastern culture area. Instead, the consumption of black drink appears to have been neither universally nor exclusively southeastern in distribution (see map 2).

CREEK CONFEDERACY

By far the most complete information on the use of black drink by any southeastern Indian group pertains to those groups who were organized into the Creek Confederacy. In a later chapter, Charles Fairbanks discusses in detail the evidence for the use of black drink by the members of the Creek Confederacy. Briefly, the Creeks consumed black drink in rigidly formalized ceremonial contexts, both as an emetic and as a highly symbolic beverage, and employed it therapeutically during curing ceremonies. In addition, early writers indicate that the men of most if not all Creek towns gathered daily in the town square or in one of their council houses to partake of black drink and to deliberate pressing matters of town business. While these meetings were more social than ceremonial, the manner in which black drink was consumed during them was still rather formalized. In these contexts the mutual consumption of black drink was taken to indicate that the drinkers were on friendly terms; the Creeks almost invariably demonstrated their peaceful intentions toward visitors by inviting them to participate in their daily black drink.[1]

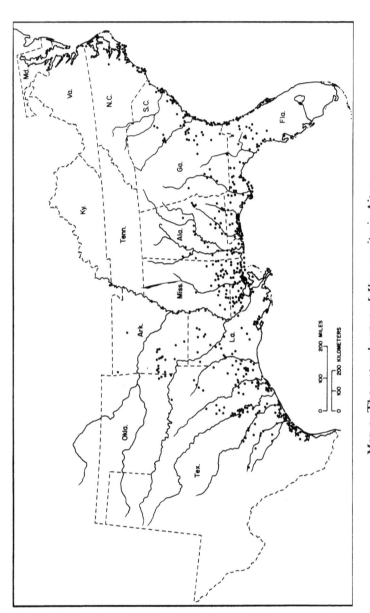

Map 1. The natural range of *Ilex vomitoria* Aiton.

This map, completed in cooperation with William C. Sturtevant, is based on distribution information associated with over four hundred herbarium sheets of *Ilex vomitoria*. The map is intended to indicate the natural range of *I. vomitoria*; collection stations of cultivated specimens were excluded from consideration. Distribution information or herbarium specimens were provided by the following individuals and the herbaria of the following institutions, to whom we express our gratitude: Delzie Demaree, Jerald T. Milanich, Gary Tucker, University of Alabama, Auburn University, University of Arkansas, University of Florida, Florida State University, University of South Florida, University of Miami, University of Georgia, Louisiana State University, Northeast Louisiana State College, University of Southwestern Louisiana, Tulane University, University of Mississippi, Mississippi State University, University of Southern Mississippi, University of North Carolina, Oklahoma State University, University of South Carolina, University of Tennessee, University of Texas, Texas A&M University, Baylor University, Southern Methodist University, Virginia Polytechnic Institute and State University, Harvard University (Gray and Arnold Arboretum Herbaria), Missouri Botanical Garden, New York Botanical Garden, Smithsonian Institution (United States National Herbarium), British Museum (Natural History), Royal Botanical Gardens (Kew), and Muséum Nationale d'Histoire Naturelle (Paris).

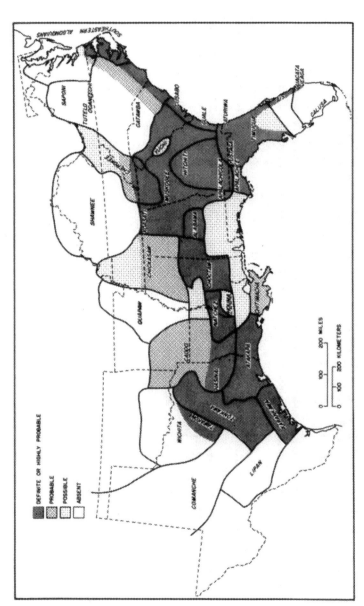

Map 2. The distribution of the use of black drink in native North America.

FLORIDA

The Calusa and other groups in the southernmost portion of Florida apparently did not prepare black drink. The absence of the drink among these groups can be attributed perhaps to their location outside the natural range of *Ilex vomitoria*. The Timucua and their neighbors, on the other hand, extensively employed *Ilex vomitoria*, not only as an important ritual beverage and emetic but as a gift offered to indicate friendly intentions.

Some of the most detailed information concerning the use of black drink by the Indians of the east coast of Florida is found in Jonathan Dickinson's narrative. Dickinson, a Quaker merchant, was shipwrecked on the east coast of Florida near Jupiter Inlet in 1699 on a voyage with his family from Port Royal, Jamaica, to Philadelphia.[2] After being held captive for five days by the Jeaga (or Jobé) Indians, who lived in the area of Jupiter Inlet, Dickinson and his party began traveling northward on their way to St. Augustine and Spanish protection.[3] Two days later they encountered the St. Lucia Indians, believed by Swanton to be the Guacata mentioned in 1575 by Fontaneda.[4] During his sojourn among the St. Lucia Indians, Dickinson observed, in the context of one of their ceremonial meetings, the manner in which they utilized black drink. In preparation for the occasion, all of the men, women, and children in the village assembled, apparently in the house of the cacique, or chief. The cacique sat at the upper end of the cabin while the other important members of the group seated themselves on a row of benches. Amidst the crying of several women, Dickinson and his group—at this point a bit anxious about the Indians' intentions toward them—heard a strange noise coming from another part of the house. Later they discovered that a man in an adjoining portion of the house was boiling a decoction of the parched leaves of the "casseena" shrub (*Ilex vomitoria*). When the "casseena," or black drink, was ready, the man dipped it out of the pot with a gourd con-

tainer and poured it into a deep bowl that held, according to
Dickinson's estimates, approximately three gallons. The man
then took the gourd dipper—described as having a long neck
with a small hole cut in the top and a larger hole in the side—
and agitated the dark brown beverage to produce a froth. The
strange noise described by Dickinson was produced by air being
forced out of the little hole on the top of the gourd when the
man pressed the dipper into the liquid. After the decoction
had cooled a bit, the cacique was presented some of it in a
shell cup. He immediately poured out a portion of it, evidently
in sacrifice, and then drank the remainder of the beverage,
afterward voicing a loud "He—m." The men seated on the
benches then began drinking their share of the decoction and
continued sipping, talking, and smoking for the better part of
the day. Only the cacique and other important men of the
group could partake of the black drink; it was strictly for-
bidden to the other men, women, and children who were
present.[5]

Sometime after this meeting, the cacique of the Ais, a neighboring group to the north, came to visit the Guacata, bearing
presents of tobacco, moss, and "some few bunches of the herb
they make their drink of." The Guacata welcomed him with
great ceremony and entertained him with drinking black drink
and smoking.[6] After a short stay with the Guacata, Dickinson
and his companions again set out northward, passing through
Ais territory just south of what is now Cape Canaveral. Here
Dickinson observed the Ais celebrating a ceremony in which
they fasted, danced, and drank black drink for three days. During this period the sick and weak members of the group received a greater portion of black drink than the others did.
Dickinson also mentions that during their council meetings
the Ais drank "casseena" and smoked from late morning or
early afternoon until evening.[7]

About 150 years before Dickinson's misfortunes, several
French explorers visited the coast of East Florida, recording
their observations and impressions of the native inhabitants.

In 1564 an expedition led by Réné Goulaine de Laudonnière reached Florida and built Fort Caroline near the mouth of the St. Johns River. The Laudonnière expedition maintained this tiny colony for a little over a year before they were overrun and expelled from Florida by Spanish forces.[8]

During their short stay in Florida, Laudonnière and his men made frequent explorations into the interior, negotiating with and observing the people they found living there. Jacques Le Moyne, a member of Laudonnière's expedition, recorded his observations of these Timucuan groups in a number of written descriptions and magnificent illustrations, later copied by Theodor De Bry in a series of engravings published in 1591. In one of these illustrations, entitled "Proceedings of the Floridians in deliberating on important affairs" (see fig. 4), Le Moyne depicts a group of men sitting in a semicircle drinking black drink from shell cups and vomiting profusely on the ground at their feet. The occasion of this assembly, according to Le Moyne, was a meeting of the chief and his advisors in a public place in the village. As the men filed in, each saluted the chief. The eldest man present saluted him first, twice lifting his hands to the height of his head and saying "Ha, he, ya, ha, ha." The rest of the group responded with "Ha, ha," and each took a seat on the bench after completing his salutation. If any important matters were to be discussed, the cacique called upon each man individually for his opinions and advice. Meanwhile he ordered the women to prepare some cassina or black drink. This they accomplished by boiling the leaves of *Ilex vomitoria*, afterward pouring the resultant decoction through a strainer. Before commencing to drink, a man asked a blessing for the chief and the other drinkers, after which the cacique was presented the hot drink in a shell cup. When the chief had drunk, he ordered the server to distribute the black drink, in the same container, to other members of the assemblage. Le Moyne observed that the use of black drink produced a diaphoretic and emetic effect and that it was taken only by those men who had proven themselves to be brave warriors.[9]

Figure 4. Eastern Timucua Indians, probably Saturiwa, taking black drink. The shell cups in the picture are incorrectly shown as nautilus snails rather than conch shells. Copy from Theodor de Bry. Bartram Museum, University of Florida.

The Timucuan consumption of black drink and their practice of inducing vomiting on ritual occasions is further documented in the early seventeenth century by Father Francisco Pareja, one of the earliest Spanish missionaries to these Indians. Interestingly, Pareja not only discusses the Indians' use of black drink but employs black drink himself as a material image in trying to convey a feeling for the subtleties of Christian theology to his Indian charges. He attempted to explicate in rather material terms the Christian concept of the multiplistic nature of God by invoking an analogy between this aspect of God and the myriad reflections emanating from the bubbles floating on the surface of the cassina.[10]

The Apalachee Indians of West Florida apparently were noted users of black drink, for the early French writers called this decoction *the des Apalaches* and *Apalachine*.[11] Yet very little is known about how the Apalachees employed black drink. Father Juan de Paina, a Spanish priest among the Apalachees during the mid-seventeenth century, describes their use of black drink in his condemnation of the annual ballgame between the Apalachee and Yustaga. The preparations preceding the actual playing of this ballgame were quite elaborate, involving bewitching, counter-bewitching, fasting, dancing, and drinking "cacina" (black drink). Several days prior to the event, a runner from the host village informed the opposing village of the date of the ballgame. At this time, the runner counted the number of people in the opposing village, gathered an equal number of small sticks, and then returned to his home village. Upon his arrival, everyone assembled and the runner bound and threw the sticks into a pot.

Then the *cacina* was ordered to be made. It could not be made from sea-coast plants, as is that which is usually drunk, but from plants coming from the forests around here. When the *cacina* arrived it was thrown into the pot with the little sticks, in the name of the players of the opposing team, in order to make them weak and without strength. If the pot should by chance be uncovered while they are playing, they would lose the game for sure.[12]

During preparations for the ballgame, the people in the host village raised the ball post into place while enacting an elaborate ritual. At this time the *usinulo,* the "Beloved Son" of the principal cacique, consecrated the post by giving it the *gua,* the salutation of the cacique, and by pouring out cassina as a sort of libation. After raising the pole, the people placed a skull or scalp at its base in memory of *Ytonanslac,* the mythical founder of the ballgame and "father" of the ball players.[13]

On the night preceding the ballgame, the cacique began to fast. At sunset or a little later, all of the players entered the council house and arranged the benches there so that they were facing in the direction of the opposing village. The fasting cacique sat behind the players' benches, where he would remain all night, advising his players of the events of the coming ballgame and admonishing them to perform to the utmost of their abilities. All the while, he smoked tobacco and drank black drink, which caused him to vomit copiously. After this purging, regardless of his physical condition upon completion of the ordeal, the cacique usually joined his fellow townsmen in the ballgame.[14]

Paina fails to mention whether the Apalachee used black drink during the actual playing of the ballgame. The black drink decoction may have been carried to the ball ground; Paina states that the pot containing it had to be covered while the game was in progress, presumably to prevent any contamination of the liquid whereby its purifying qualities would have been weakened or destroyed.[15]

The use of black drink by the Apalachees possibly differs in at least one important detail from that of the other southeastern Indian groups who employed it. Paina mentions only three persons using the cassina—the runner, the *usinulo,* and the cacique, with the cacique alone consuming it—implying that the Apalachees' use of black drink was limited to these special individuals. Paina does make the tantalizing statement that the cassina used at the ballgame preparation ceremony "could not be made from sea-coast plants, as is that which is usually drunk, but from plants coming from the forests around here." This implies that the Apalachees supplemented their local supply of cassina with *Ilex vomitoria* from the coast for use on occasions other than the ballgame ceremony. If so, it is possible that on these other occasions black drink was employed less esoterically. On the other hand, there is the remote possibility that Paina was describing how the neighboring Timucuan groups or the Spanish prepared their black drink, using this observation as a comparison to the Apalachees' mode of preparation and employment of cassina during their ballgame. If the latter is true, then perhaps only the special officials utilized cassina, and they only during the ballgame ceremony.

In more recent times, the Seminoles, a mélange of eighteenth-century emigrants into Florida from Georgia and Alabama, have celebrated a ceremony comparable in style and intent to the Creek busk in which they prepared an emetic concoction called the "Big Gathered Medicine." In the early 1950s William C. Sturtevant recorded that this concoction contained as many as fifteen different plants, but *Ilex vomitoria* was not one of them.[16] By this date Seminole territory was entirely south of the natural range of this species.

COASTAL GEORGIA

Because very little ethnohistorical information exists in the published record for the Indian groups who inhabited the coastal regions of Georgia, it is impossible to determine whether all of them prepared black drink. Certainly *Ilex vomitoria* was available for their use since it grows in profusion along the Georgia coast. In the early sixteenth century, Peter Martyr, one of the earliest historians of the New World, described what may have been the use of *I. vomitoria* by the Chicora and Duhare Indians, whom John R. Swanton identifies as either the Guale or Cusabo living along the coast of Georgia.[17] On the basis of information supplied by Francisco Chicorana, a

Chicora Indian whom he interviewed in Spain, Martyr reports that the Indians of Chicora and Duhare drank a decoction of a plant called *guahi* or ate the herb itself to induce vomiting and thereby relieve the discomfort of "a bilious stomach."[18] Swanton suggests that this plant may have been *Ilex vomitoria,* but it cannot be definitely identified.[19]

Around 1595 Fray Andrés de San Miguel described the use of cassina by the Guale Indians living near the present location of St. Simons Island, Georgia. After parching the cassina leaves in an earthenware pot, the Guale added water and brought the decoction to a boil. While it was still boiling, they drew some of it off and drank it hot. San Miguel also observed the use of this drink by the Guale in a particular ceremony which was open only to the leading men of the town. In preparation for this ritual, the Guale brewed a large supply of black drink, which they poured into one large pot, as well as into a number of smaller jars of two different types. When the ceremony began, a man took a jar of each type and presented them to the other participants, who were seated on a long bench. Each man drank until his abdomen became distended. After a short while everyone regurgitated copious amounts of the drink while other individuals, on their knees, spread the liquid in all directions with their hands. This marked the conclusion of the ceremony. San Miguel was told that the emetic effect of the cassina came about by the addition of sea water. He doubted the authenticity of this report since he knew of a Guale chief, named Don Felipe, who vomited every time he drank cassina even though no brine was included. San Miguel also mentions that the Guale employed cassina therapeutically as a diuretic to prevent kidney stones.[20]

In 1722 Fray Pedro Muñoz mentioned the Guale's use of black drink in his description of the hardships of an unnamed Spanish religious official who was the sole survivor of a Guale raid on the Spanish missions in their province. The Guale had enslaved this unfortunate Spaniard, forcing him to perform several menial tasks including fetching the water required to prepare their cassina.[21]

PIEDMONT AND COASTAL CAROLINAS AND VIRGINIA

Extensive groves of *Ilex vomitoria* can be seen flourishing today along the coast and outer banks of North Carolina. Similar
stands of this shrub were observed over two centuries ago by
such travelers as William Byrd and John Lawson.[22] Lawson
wrote in the early eighteenth century that he had discovered
at least two if not three types of yaupon (*Ilex vomitoria*) growing on the coast and islands of Carolina.[23] The coastal Carolina
Indians, according to Lawson, employed two methods of
parching or "curing" their yaupon ("call'd by the South-
Carolina Indians, Cassena") prior to making a tea with it. In
the first of these, the Indians initially bruised the leaves and
small twigs in a mortar, then transferred them to an earthenware vessel over a fire until the yaupon was parched. Using the
second procedure, other groups bruised the yaupon leaves and
twigs as before, but in this method they filled the bottom of a
bowl with live coals over which they placed the yaupon. After
the leaves and twigs were parched, the Indians spread them
out on mats in the sun to dry.

According to Lawson, all of the coastal Carolina Indians
made a tea from the yaupon tree, the foliage of which they
traded to the inland "Westward Indians" for considerable
profit.[24] In fact, Lawson states that the Carolina Indians venerated *Ilex vomitoria* to a greater degree than any of the other
plants with which they were acquainted. He also relates the
Indians' version of how the usefulness of the plant was discovered. According to this story, an Indian man had been
plagued by a lingering illness that none of the Indian doctors
could cure. One day he fell asleep and dreamed that if he took
a decoction of the tree that grew at his head, he would be
cured. When he awoke he discovered the "*Yaupon* or *Cassena-
Tree*" growing there even though it had not been there when
he had fallen asleep. The man followed the directions of his
dream and was quickly cured.[25]

John Brickell, another early resident of North Carolina, also discusses the use of black drink by the Carolina Indians. Although Brickell frequently plagiarized Lawson, he does provide some descriptions of the use of black drink that are not supplied by the earlier writer. For example, he reports that the Indians celebrated a victory over their enemies with feasts that lasted several days, during which time they drank great quantities of yaupon tea. When their war expeditions were less successful, the Indians held a different ceremony to remind the people of their ancestors who had perished at the hands of their enemies. When everyone had assembled, a man who had been previously selected struck the chief's favorite son three times with a weapon. In the intervals between blows, this man presented the chief with food or black drink. On the third blow the chief's son fell to the ground, at which time a number of people rushed to his side and began to wail. During this time, the chief and his advisors feasted in silence until night. The ceremony ended with joyous dancing and singing. Brickell also mentions that the Indians drank *"Cassena"* during council meetings and burial ceremonies and that they took it medicinally for its emetic and diuretic properties.[26]

Mark Catesby, a naturalist of the early eighteenth century, concluded that the Indians' great demand for *Ilex vomitoria* arose from its virtue as a medicine rather than from its use as a beverage, since it seemed to him to be "as little agreeable to an *Indian* as to a *European* Palate." He reports that the maritime Indians supplied those in the mountains and to the north and west with it. Catesby also describes an annual spring ceremony in which the Indians ritually drank black drink. In this ceremony, after everyone had purged their homes by burning all their old furnishings, they assembled at the town house to observe the celebration. First the chief was served black drink in a previously unused bowl or marine shell by the person next to him in social rank. The drinking followed the lines of the social hierarchy down to but apparently not including the women and children.[27] Catesby fails to attribute these various uses of black drink to any particular southeastern Indian group. He spent almost three years in Carolina and adjacent regions and probably observed black drink in use among a number of different groups. More than likely his account is a synthesis of these observations.

Moses A. Curtis, quoting an unidentified source, describes a ceremony in which certain unspecified inland groups made an annual pilgrimage to the coast from a distance of some hundred miles to secure a supply of the yaupon leaves. While on the coast, these Indians prepared a large quantity of black drink, drinking it from a bowl that held about a pint. They continued drinking and vomiting for two or three days, until they were thoroughly purged; and they returned home, with everyone taking a bundle of the shrub with them.[28]

Although none of these early writers refers to any particular Carolina coastal or piedmont group by name, the majority of these Indians probably prepared and drank black drink on one occasion or another.[29] *Ilex vomitoria* was locally available to many of these groups, and Lawson mentions that the coastal groups traded it to those located inland. In his discussion of the Machapunga Indians of North Carolina, Speck mentions that yaupon was still used in 1916 as a regular beverage and medicine by the mixed-blood inhabitants of Roanoke Island, the adjacent sand islands, and the mainland counties of Dare and Hyde.[30] Because of extensive racial and cultural intermixing on North Carolina's coast, the use of black drink in this context cannot be considered purely Indian in derivation. In fact, the white inhabitants of North Carolina's outer banks have adopted yaupon tea as their own and for the most part are only vaguely aware of its Indian origins.[31] However, the fact that these white people use the coastal North Carolina Indian term *yaupon* for the plant rather than the English term *black drink* or the Spanish appellation *cacina* suggests that they originally adopted it from these Indians rather than discovering it on their own or learning of it from the Spanish or other Indian groups located farther to the south.

Speck also suggests that the modern Catawba medicinal *Crotalaria sagittalis* or *C. rotundifolia* (commonly known in English as "Rattle Box") is equivalent to the southeastern

black drink, but it is difficult to see how he arrived at this conclusion. The Catawba employed this plant exclusively as a
remedy for "mental troubles," and Speck did not discover any
more ritualized use for it. In fact, the only similarity between
Rattle Box and *Ilex vomitoria* is that both materials turn black
when used as infusions.[32]

By earliest colonial times, the Virginia Tidewater area was
inhabited by a number of Indian groups known collectively
today as the Virginia Algonquians. To their west lived several
Siouan-speaking groups (including the Saponi, Tutelo, and
Ocaneechi encountered by John Lawson in his travels), with
whom many of the Virginia Algonquian groups maintained
hostile relations. Although these groups are reported to have
employed a wide range of plants to induce emesis, none of the
early writers mentions that the coastal Algonquians or the interior Siouan groups utilized black drink as an emetic or ceremonial beverage.[33] This absence is relatively understandable
for the Siouan groups, since they were located some distance
from the natural range of *Ilex vomitoria* and separated from
it by hostile groups. The coastal Algonquians, on the other
hand, probably had a readily available supply of yaupon, since
Ilex vomitoria presently reaches the northern limits of its distribution around the mouth of the Chesapeake Bay in Nor-
folk, Princess Anne, and Northampton counties (see map 1).
Because of this and because of their close linguistic and cultural affiliations with Algonquian-speaking groups on the Carolina coast, who employed black drink on a regular basis, it
seems likely that at least some of the Virginia Algonquians
would have prepared black drink.

CHEROKEES

Like most other southeastern Indian groups, the Cherokees
traditionally believed that the success or failure of many under-
takings was directly related to the degree of physical and

spiritual purity maintained by the individuals who endeavored to perform them. Accordingly, they resorted to the consumption of emetic plants and decoctions to purify themselves on those occasions when such a state of purity was demanded. The Cherokees employed emetic decoctions in a number of contexts, perhaps the most notable of these being their green corn ceremonies, rituals preceding and following raiding expeditions, curing ceremonies, and ceremonies performed prior to playing a ballgame. Although the plants included in these emetic decoctions often remain unidentified, particularly in the earlier reports, it appears that the ceremonial use of black drink by the Cherokees traditionally has been of much less importance than their utilization of decoctions prepared from a number of other plants.[34]

During the colonial period the Cherokees occupied a number of towns in adjacent portions of the present states of Georgia, South Carolina, North Carolina, and Tennessee. In this locality they were situated far to the interior of the natural range of *Ilex vomitoria*. Their apparent failure to employ black drink to any significant degree perhaps can be attributed in part to the absence of a naturally available local supply of the plant. However, there is some indication that the Cherokees transplanted *Ilex vomitoria* into their rather mountainous habitat and therefore presumably employed it on some occasions. The earliest evidence for the Cherokees' transplantation of this plant is found on a herbarium sheet of *Ilex vomitoria* presently housed in the general herbarium of the British Museum (Natural History). On the reverse side of this sheet is the notation, in a very clear eighteenth-century hand, that this specimen was collected in 1769 by W. V. Turner in "Cherroke countrey" and that the Indian name for this plant was "Cowwta Oucoroge." Turner did not note the exact location in Cherokee territory where he collected this specimen. However, it may be that he obtained it at or near one of the Lower Cherokee towns (located where the present states of North Carolina, South Carolina, and Georgia converge), since the /r/ phoneme appears only in the Lower Cherokee dialect of the language.[35]

William Bartram, an eighteenth-century naturalist from Philadelphia, provides more concrete evidence that the inhabitants of the Cherokee settlements to the west of the Lower Cherokee towns also transplanted *Ilex vomitoria*. While traveling through Cherokee country in 1775, Bartram observed a carefully pruned and cultivated grove of "Casine yapon" (an early designation for *Ilex vomitoria*) growing near Jore, a Cherokee town in western North Carolina, near the Georgia border. The Indians called this shrub "the beloved tree" and drank a strong infusion prepared from its leaves, buds, and tender branches. According to Bartram, it was "venerated by the Creeks and all the Southern maritime nations of Indians," but he fails to indicate for what purposes the Cherokees employed it.[36] John P. Brown notes that Nancy Ward, a beloved woman of the Cherokees in the mid-eighteenth century, had as one of her duties the preparation of the "sacred black drink," which the warriors took before leaving on a raiding expedition.[37] However, Brown does not state that this black drink was prepared from *Ilex vomitoria;* he may be employing the term to refer to ceremonial decoctions in general. In any case, it is obvious that the Cherokees transplanted the *Ilex vomitoria* shrubs that Bartram observed at Jore, since this town was located a great distance from where *I. vomitoria* naturally occurs. On the other hand, the practice of transplanting may not have been widespread among the Cherokees, since Bartram notes that this was the only place in the Cherokee country where he saw the plant growing.[38]

YUCHIS

In the early eighteenth century the Yuchis inhabited the banks of the Savannah River above the present Augusta, Georgia. Speaking a language remotely related to Siouan, they claimed to have been one of the original groups to inhabit the South-east.[39] However, in the historic period they were allied with the Muskogean-speaking groups who constituted the Creek Confederacy.

The Yuchis often employed emetics to purify themselves before any serious undertaking, such as going to war or to hunt and during curing ceremonies, as well as in their annual town ceremonies. But no information exists that would indicate that the Yuchis ever used *Ilex vomitoria* as an ingredient in any of their emetic preparations. It seems likely that the Yuchis would have prepared black drink at least occasionally because of their close ties with the groups in the Creek Confederacy, all of whom apparently employed black drink. Moreover, the fact that the Salzburgers in early eighteenth-century Georgia drank cassina implies that the Yuchis, with whom they had relations, also used it.[40] On the other hand, whatever importance, if any, they may have ascribed to *I. vomitoria* probably would have been overshadowed by the importance that they attached to two other plants, button snakeroot and redroot. The use of these two plants as emetics and purifiers was central to the performance of many of the Yuchi rituals and crucial to their existence as a people. According to Yuchi mythology, the Sun instructed them to drink a concoction made from button snakeroot and redroot in their annual town ceremonies to purify themselves against sickness in the ensuing year. If they discontinued these ceremonies, they believed the Sun would set in the east and the world would come to an end.[41]

ALABAMAS

Jean-Bernard Bossu traveled through the Alabama territory in 1759, leaving an account of various customs and ceremonies of the Alabama Indians. Concerning the Alabamas' use of black drink in their decision-making assemblies, Bossu says:

All the Savages of the country of the Alibamons drink *cassine;* it is the leaf of an extremely bushy shrub; it is not larger than a black poplar [*liard*], but denticulated all around the circumference. They brown it like we make coffee, & drink the infusion with many ceremonies. When this diuretic drink is made, the young men [*gens*] go to present it in calabashes open in the manner of cups, according to the quality & the rank of the Chiefs, and of the Warriors: that is to say, to the Esteemed ones, then to the other warriors, according to their grade. They observe the same order, when they present the calumet for smoking; while you drink, they howl in a loud voice, & diminish by gradation; when you have ceased to drink, they get their breath, & when you recommence they continue the same howling. This sort of orgy lasts sometimes for six hours in the morning until 2 hours after noon. These Savages are never otherwise indisposed by their drink, to which they attribute many virtues. They return it without efforts & without difficulty.

The women never drink of this beverage made for the warriors alone.[42]

In addition to using cassina in their decision-making assemblies, the Alabamas employed it as a symbol of peace. According to Bossu, during the French colonial administration, a young Alabama man killed a French soldier and escaped to a neighboring tribe. When the French demanded that the murder be revenged, the Alabama leaders extricated their tribesman from his sanctuary and brought him to the French for trial. At the trial the French insisted that justice be accomplished, so the Alabamas killed the offender by clubbing him on the head. After the execution the Alabamas made peace with the French by offering them the calumet and cassina.[43]

Bossu also notes that the Alabamas used *Ilex vomitoria* medicinally as a diuretic and that a strong dose of it would cause a patient to shiver for a short time.[44] John R. Swanton, in a list of Alabama medicines collected in Texas and Oklahoma and published in 1928, states that the Alabamas' *kàtsgimilpa* (translated as "catfish eat it" or "catfish food") actually was *Ilex vomitoria*. He did not find the Alabamas using it for any strictly medicinal purpose, although "it was daily employed by the old people in early days to clear out the system and produce ceremonial purity."[45]

CHICKASAWS

The Chickasaws, a Muskogean-speaking people, lived in northern Mississippi, western Tennessee, and western Kentucky until their removal west of the Mississippi between 1822 and 1838. One of the best sources of information about the customs of the Chickasaws in the early historical period is James Adair, an enterprising trader who lived among various southeastern Indian groups for over thirty years, spending twenty-four of these years off and on with the Chickasaws in northern Mississippi. Adair produced a very detailed description of the customs and practices of the southeastern groups that he knew, including the Cherokee, Creek, Choctaw, and Chickasaw; unfortunately he tended to obscure tribal lines in his attempt to prove that the American Indians in general were descended from the ten lost tribes of Israel.

Adair frequently mentions the use of black drink and other ceremonial beverages in his discussions, but it is difficult to determine exactly to which groups he is referring. For example, in his description of the victory ceremonies following the return of a Chickasaw war party from Illinois in 1765, Adair mentions that the *yahola* or black drink cry (which he interprets as being "Yo He Wah," synonymous with the Hebrew Yahweh or Jehovah) accompanying these celebrations varied a bit from "their established method of invoking YO HE WAH, when they are drinking their bitter drink (the *Cusseena*) in their temples."[46] In this statement, Adair could be referring either to a specifically Chickasaw practice or to a custom of any or all of the other southeastern Indian groups with which he was familiar. Similarly, in a discussion of the flora in the Chickasaw territory, Adair states that the "Yopon, or Cusseena" tree grew as far as the salt air reaches over the lowlands, that it was very agreeable once a person was accustomed to it, and that it cured a tremor in the nerves.[47] Again, even though he is discussing the Chickasaw here, Adair does not state specifically that they used this decoction.

Adair reports that the Indians (probably the Creeks) employed black drink on every religious occasion of the year and that some of the old men drank this and other bitter decoctions to purge themselves severely. He also mentions that the southeastern Indians in general drank black drink when making peace, but when readying for war they consumed a war physic prepared from button snakeroot.[48] In addition he provides an extensive description of the use of black drink and other ceremonial beverages in the green corn ceremony—in fact, the most detailed description extant from the early writers—but this discussion appears to be a synthesis of his observations of this ceremony as practiced by the Creeks, Cherokees, and possibly the Chickasaws.[49] In light of the fact that he spent such an extended period of time with the Chickasaws, one might suppose that he was presenting an account of a Chickasaw ceremony. Yet, the only extant description of the performance of this ceremony by the Chickasaws is the one collected by Frank G. Speck during fieldwork in Indian Territory in the early twentieth century. In his discussion of this ceremony, Speck states that the people gathered together on one day, took an emetic made from redroot, and then ate a feast of fresh roasted ears of corn.[50] It seems unlikely that all other early writers would have remained silent on a ceremony obviously so important as the green corn ceremony if the Chickasaws in fact celebrated it. Swanton believes that if the Chicksaws had such a ceremony, they borrowed it from the Creeks and later abandoned it.[51] If so, it is highly probable that the Chickasaws drank black drink at least during the period when they performed this ceremony, since the consumption of black drink was a central component of the Creek ceremony.

CHOCTAWS

Victor Tixier, a young French adventurer who traveled through Louisiana in 1840, makes passing reference to the use of black drink by the Choctaws in Louisiana. While visiting at the plantation of Pierre Sauve, twenty miles north of New Orleans, Tixier encountered a group of Choctaws who had abandoned their village on the Red River to spend the winter months in southern Louisiana. After these Choctaws departed from M. Sauve's plantation to return to their Red River village, Tixier discovered that they had left the bones of their dead in a nearby cemetery. Anxious to view these graves, Tixier, with the owner of the property on which the burial ground was located and a black slave, set out to examine them. On the way, the planter warned Tixier that the Choctaws on their return would discover that the burials had been disturbed and would engage in their "medicine" to divine what had become of the bones that Tixier planned to remove. The planter added, "They will guess you were the one who opened their tombs, but it remains to be seen whether truth will be revealed by the juice of *cassine* they will drink or by information cleverly gathered."[52]

The "juice of *cassine*" mentioned here by the planter apparently was a decoction of *Ilex vomitoria* since *cassine* is a common name for that plant. From the description it appears that these Choctaws employed black drink for divinatory purposes.[53] Sixty-nine years later, in 1909, David Bushnell observed that the Choctaws of Bayou Lacomb, St. Tammany Parish, had no remembrance of ever having prepared a tea from "*Ilex cassine*" (*I. vomitoria* Ait.?), even though this species of holly grows throughout their region.[54] On the other hand, in 1922 Bushnell learned that a group of Indians who had lived near the south shore of Lake Pontchartrain had at one time prepared a beverage from the dried or green leaves of the yaupon tree (*Ilex vomitoria*), which they drank like ordinary tea, adding milk when it was available. Bushnell gained this information from the last remaining member of the group and was unable to establish a definite tribal identity for them; however, he believed they were of Muskogean stock closely allied with the Choctaws inhabiting the northern shore of Lake Pontchartrain.[55]

In 1775 Bernard Romans described a plant employed by the

Choctaws in their rainmaking ceremonies which might have been *Ilex vomitoria*. The Choctaw rainmakers assembled in a deserted field and boiled the plant in a large pot around which they danced and sang. If rain soon followed, the rainmakers boasted of the efficacy of the plant, but if no precipitation occurred, they claimed that they had not made the physic strong enough. The Choctaw reportedly referred to this plant as *Esta Hoola* or "the most beloved," and, although he could not make a definite identification of the plant, Romans reports that he saw two "species" of it.[56]

It cannot be concluded with any certainty that the Choctaws were employing *Ilex vomitoria* in this particular ceremony, since Romans was not more explicit in his description of the plant in question. The Choctaw name for the plant, glossed by Romans as "the most beloved," is strongly reminiscent of the term "the beloved tree," which Bartram claims was employed by the Indians to refer to *Ilex vomitoria*. In addition, Romans's observation of two distinct species of the plant echoes Lawson's report that two if not three types of yaupon grew on the coast and outer banks of North Carolina.[57] However, no other southeastern groups are known to have utilized *I. vomitoria* in such a fashion, and Romans does not report that the Choctaw rainmakers consumed their decoction, as might be expected if it had been black drink.

LOWER MISSISSIPPI VALLEY

The use of black drink is suspected to have been fairly widespread among the Indian groups of the Lower Mississippi Valley, but definite accounts of this use exist only for the Chitimacha and Natchez. The paucity of evidence relating to the employment of *Ilex vomitoria* by the Indian groups of this area derives in large part from the fact that much of the information compiled on these groups during the French and Spanish colonial periods remains unpublished in the archives of Europe and North America. Undoubtedly, future examinations of such unpublished ethnographic materials will reveal additional information on the use of black drink by the Indian groups of the Lower Mississippi.

According to Chitimacha texts collected by Albert S. Gatschet in Charenton, Louisiana, between December 1881 and January 1882, the Chitimacha held curing ceremonies in which a shaman stupefied himself by drinking a decoction of "pounded cassine" (*nuait to"hmina*) and smoking cigars made from cassina and *apopua* (possibly *Lobelia inflata* L.). The shaman remained unconscious for about two hours, during which time he attempted to discover if his patient would die.[58] Such procedures seem to have been characteristic of Chitimacha shamanistic performances. In fact, Gatschet suggests that the Chitimacha term for conjurer or shaman (*Ka'tchmish*) derived from *ka'tchit*, "to drink," because the Chitimacha shamans induced their divinatory stupors by drinking an infusion of cassina leaves.[59] Yet there is some basis for questioning Gatschet's identification of *nuait* as cassina if, as seems likely, he was employing the term *cassine* to refer to *Ilex vomitoria*. None of the other Indian groups in the Southeast who were familiar with *Ilex vomitoria* are reported to have smoked it. Furthermore, with the possible exception of the Choctaws' utilization of cassina for divinatory purposes, the employment of a decoction prepared from *Ilex vomitoria* to produce an unconscious state is not otherwise documented. Gatschet possibly was mistaken in his identification of *nuait* as cassina, or perhaps *apopua* rather than cassina produced the dramatic results he reports.

Some support for the validity of Gatschet's identification is supplied by John R. Swanton, who between 1908 and 1931 revised Gatschet's unpublished Chitimacha dictionary with the assistance of Benjamin Paul, a Chitimacha from Charenton, Louisiana. Swanton maintains, with Gatschet, that the Chitimacha shamans both smoked and drank cassina (the Chitimacha term for which he renders as *wai't'i*) to bring on stuporous states. However, it is impossible to determine if Swanton independently collected his information concerning cassina or if he derived it from Gatschet's fieldnotes. Swanton also lists another plant, *nai'k'a*, with which the Chitimacha shamans prepared a drink. This decoction produced a sleep in which the shamans divined a cure for their patients' maladies. Swanton did not secure an identification for *nai'k'a* and Benjamin Paul knew nothing about it.[60]

La Page du Pratz, a Frenchman in Louisiana during the early eighteenth century, states that the Natchez Indians prepared a war drink from the "leaves of the Apalachine."[61] According to Charlevoix, "Apalachina" is a French synonym for cassina (presumably *Ilex vomitoria*) and is derived from the name of the Apalachee Indians of Florida, "from whom the Spaniards learned the use of this plant."[62] In 1730 Père le Petit reported that the Natchez prepared their war medicine from an unidentified root boiled in large kettles full of water. Each warrior drank two pots of the medicine, which caused immediate and copious vomiting.[63]

In 1772 David Taitt visited with a group of Natchez who were living among the Abihka Creeks in Alabama after being forced from their homelands by the French in the 1730s. When Taitt arrived, the headmen of the Natchez village welcomed him into their square, where they conversed, smoked tobacco, and drank black drink.[64] Whether the Natchez used black drink in a similar context prior to their assimilation into the Creek Confederacy is not known. Because no other writers observed the Natchez using black drink in welcoming and entertaining visitors, it may be that they adopted this practice after their relocation among the Creeks.

Paul du Ru, a Jesuit missionary and chaplain on Lemoyne d'Iberville's second expedition, observed a most interesting custom while visiting the Houma Indians of Louisiana in 1700. Apparently du Ru arrived at the Houma village in the midst of a funeral ceremony, possibly held in behalf of a chief who had died some time before. At daybreak a group of mourners began to wail and were joined by a singer who performed a dirge over the dead man's tomb while perfuming it with tobacco. This ceremony lasted about thirty minutes and was followed by a formal breakfast, during which the people continued to mourn. After the meal a group of women, including some of the dead chief's wives, began to spin and weave bark in a cabin. After they had worked for some time the women began to weep again, while one of their number went outside to boil a large pot of water into which she placed a handful of an unidentified herb noted for its emetic properties. She then brought the decoction into the house, and the other women began to drink it. As soon as they had regurgitated the liquid, the women ceased their weeping and cleared all of the offerings from the grave of the dead man, evidently ending the mourning ceremony.[65] While the Houma women described by du Ru definitely were employing a plant emetic of some sort in addition to water, it is impossible to determine if this plant was *Ilex vomitoria*. Frank G. Speck, while investigating the ethnic relationships of the Houma in southern Louisiana during 1937 and 1938, discovered that the modern Houma had no knowledge of *Ilex vomitoria*, and he does not list any other substances that the Houma employed as emetics.[66]

TRANS-MISSISSIPPI

The earliest reference to the use of a beverage presumed to be black drink is found in the *Relation of Alvar Nuñez Cabeça de Vaca*, first published in 1542. While traveling along the east coast of Texas in the early sixteenth century, Cabeça de Vaca encountered several groups who were drinking a tea prepared from the leaves of a tree that to him resembled an oak.[67] He reports that the Indians first parched the leaves in a pot over a fire and then poured water into the pot to boil the decoction. While the drink was boiling, the vessel was kept carefully covered to prevent contamination by any passing females. When it had boiled twice, the Indians cooled the drink in a gourd container and produced a thick yellowish froth on top by stirring it or pouring it from container to container. They then took the liquid from the pot and drank it as hot as they could stand it, all the while yelling a cry that Cabeça de Vaca interpreted as "Who wishes to drink?"[68] When this cry began, all females froze in place and refrained from making any movement until the drinking was completed. If a woman violated this restriction, the men punished her severely and threw away the decoction that they had prepared. Cabeça de Vaca also mentions that if such a violation occurred, the men easily vomited any of the decoction that they had drunk. This regurgitation process may have been the desired effect of drinking the decoction as well as a reaction to a fear of pollution incurred from drinking the now-contaminated decoction. During this ceremony the men fasted for three days, and daily each one drank 1½ arrobas (approximately 6⅜ gallons, wine measure) of the decoction.[69]

Cabeça de Vaca implies that this description is a generalized account of how a number of groups used this preparation. These groups included the Cahoques, Han, Churruco, Doguenes, Mendica, Quevenes, Mariames, Guaycones, Yguazes, Atayos, Acubadaos, Quitoks, Chavavares, Maliacones, Cultalchulches, Susolas, Comos, Camoles, and the "People of the Figs." Unfortunately these names do not correspond to more modern names for groups in this area; hence a definite identification of them cannot be given. Swanton believes that at least one of these groups, the Atayos, was identical with either the Toho or Tahaha, both Tonkawan bands. The other groups probably were bands of Atakapan, Karankawan, Tonkawan, and Coahuiltecan speakers.[70]

Although the groups described by Cabeça de Vaca cannot be definitely identified, groups known to be living in this same area at the time of Cabeça de Vaca's visit were observed in later times drinking black drink. Simars de Bellisle, a young French officer, was abandoned along with four other men near St. Bernard's Bay on the Gulf of Mexico in the early 1700s. After his companions had perished, Bellisle encountered a band of Atakapa Indians, who captured and enslaved him. During his captivity among the Atakapa, Bellisle observed that in inclement weather the usual search for food was discontinued.

Instead everyone stayed inside for two or three days, eating no food and drinking only water, which they regurgitated with ease. The Atakapas attributed some beneficial effect to this purging, and, because this regurgitation process supposedly allayed hunger as well, an infusion of *Ilex vomitoria* or a similar plant may have been involved rather than water alone.[71] In 1762 Jean-Bernard Bossu related a glorified version of Bellisle's adventures and, in a footnote to his description of this episode, mentioned that the Atakapa were cannibals who feasted on the flesh of their war captives but ordinarily subsisted on fish and drank cassina.[72] J. O. Dyer states in 1917 that the Lake Charles Atakapa in Louisiana prepared yaupon tea as a beverage and that they may have used it at certain times during the year to cleanse the system.[73]

The Karankawa Indians of the Gulf coast of Texas drank black drink in a celebration held at the time of each full moon and after a very successful hunting or fishing expedition. In 1891 Alice W. Oliver, who had been intimately acquainted with the Karankawas during her childhood in Texas, described this ceremony (which she called a "fandango"). According to Oliver, a group of Indians assembled in a tent and boiled yaupon tea in a vessel on the central fire. During the preparation process the Indians occasionally stirred the decoction with a whisk until a yellowish froth covered the top. Then they passed the vessel among the group members who were seated in a circle around the inside of the tent, and each participant drank freely. After consuming black drink the group began to dance and continued the celebration until the morning of the next day. On the second day everyone slept and relaxed. Oliver states that the decoction used in this ceremony was very bitter and was said to have been intoxicating, although she doubted the latter since it produced no visible effects in the drinkers. This report of intoxication may have derived from the fact that the Karankawas substituted whiskey for yaupon tea when it was available.[74]

Located to the north and west of the Karankawas in aboriginal times were approximately twenty-five distinct groups organized into three or more confederations and referred to collectively as the Caddo. Originally inhabiting large sections of the present states of Louisiana, Arkansas, Oklahoma, and Texas, these Caddoan groups interacted with groups in the Southeast as well as with those in the Prairies, the Plains, and northeastern Mexico.[75]

Early Spanish accounts document that the members of the Hasinai Confederacy (the largest of the Caddoan confederacies) consumed black drink on several different ritual occasions. During the early decades of the eighteenth century, Fray Isidro Felis de Espinosa described the Hasinais' employment of black drink during the performance of their harvest festival. The Hasinai celebrated this ceremony during the new moon in September, after they had harvested their crops. Six days before the first day of the ceremony, the men gathered at the house of the chief, where the elders prayed and distributed "the warm drinks of foamy laurel tea."[76] Fray Juan Agustín de Morfi states that this tea was *cazina* (black drink), as does another Spanish priest, Fray Francisco Hidalgo, who says that it was a tea similar to that commonly used in Florida.[77]

Espinosa relates that the Hasinai also drank the laurel tea in their *sacabbi* (forecasting ceremony) held during the new moon in February. This ceremony was for the purpose of foretelling the events of the coming year, especially in relation to the success of their harvests and the abundance of game. According to Espinosa, when all the people had gathered together, the medicine men entered the principal house and began brewing a tea made from laurel leaves. Morfi seemingly equates this decoction with *cassina,* implying that the "laurel" referred to here actually was *Ilex vomitoria.*[78] The shamans drank this tea all morning, occasionally offering drinks of it to the chiefs. After praying, dancing, and offering tobacco to the fire, the shamans made public their prophecies for the year.[79]

At least one and possibly two other groups inhabiting territory outside the Southeast, to the west and south of these Caddoan groups, employed black drink. Jean Louis Berlandier, a young French biologist and member of a surveying and scientific expedition sent from Mexico City to Texas in 1827, reports that the Tawakoni (a Wichita tribe), along with the Caddo and Karankawa, frequently prepared a tealike infusion from the leaves of a plant known as *té del indio* or *chocolate del indio,* which they drank after heating and skimming it. Berlandier identified this plant as a member of the Rhamnaceae family, but more recent investigators, using Berlandier's herbarium specimens, have identified it as *Ilex vomitoria.* According to Berlandier, these Indians employed black drink medicinally as a pectoral, and the Texas women, both Indian and white, drank it to bring on suppressed menses.[80] Berlandier later reports that the Tonkawa also employed black drink (*té del indio*) as a medicinal, but he contradicts his earlier statement concerning the Tawakonis' use of black drink by claiming that the Tawakonis, along with the Comanches and Lipan Apaches, never used it.[81] Whether both the Tonkawa and Tawakoni or the Tonkawa alone were employing black drink, the distribution of the use of black drink apparently reaches its western limits here. These limits essentially coincide with the western boundaries of the distribution of *Ilex vomitoria.*

The use of black drink by these Texas Indian groups bears very little resemblance to the use of this decoction by the southeastern Indians. The absence of substantial southeastern influence on the ways in which these groups utilized black drink is indicated in part by the fact that Indian women in this area were allowed to employ black drink; in the Southeast, women usually were restricted from using it. In addition, the Tonkawa and Tawakoni apparently employed black drink only as a medicinal; their informal and rather limited use of this decoction contrasts with the multiplicity of highly ritualized roles for which the southeastern Indians employed black drink.

SUMMARY AND CONCLUSIONS

The uneven and unsystematic ethnographic coverage of the Southeast and adjacent regions renders impossible the completion of any truly definitive survey of the use of black drink in native North America. Yet the information available at present provides unimpeachable documentation of the widespread popularity enjoyed by black drink among those Indian groups who had access to the *Ilex vomitoria* plant. While not all southeastern Indian groups are known to have prepared and consumed black drink, most if not all the groups who inhabited the areas where *Ilex vomitoria* natively occurs evidently employed this decoction. Furthermore, in those parts of the Southeast where this plant is not naturally available, it often was acquired through trade or transplantation.

The utilization of black drink has been unquestionably documented in the Southeast for the groups in the Creek Confederacy (including the Alabama and Apalachicola), as well as for the Timucua, Guacata, Ais, Apalachee, Guale, the coastal Carolina groups, Cherokee, Choctaw, Natchez, Atakapa, Karankawa, and certain of the Caddoan groups. In addition, the groups along the Gulf coast and adjacent Lower Mississippi Valley along with the Chickasaw, Yuchi, and some of the more southerly Virginia Algonquians probably prepared black drink at one time or another in their past. There also is a possibility that the Seminole and some of the piedmont Carolina Indians employed black drink on occasion, but the evidence for their use of it is tenuous at best. There is no reason to believe that the majority of Indian groups in the subtropical regions of Florida or the piedmont of Virginia employed black drink on any occasion, although they may have been familiar with it through contacts with other groups that did. Black drink was also used in areas outside the Southeast proper. In the interior of Texas, the Tonkawa and probably the Tawakoni prepared black drink, but these groups apparently failed to imbue black drink with the symbolic import associated with its use in the Southeast.

The evidence presented here indicates that most southeastern Indian groups did not consider black drink to be an ordinary tea that could be consumed by anyone at any time. Instead they viewed it as an esoteric preparation and generally restricted its use to special contexts or to special individuals within the larger social universe. Many groups employed black drink only in conjunction with male activities, and in some cases only the men of greatest prestige were allowed to consume it. In addition, while the consumption of black drink often took place in ceremonial contexts, a number of southeastern Indian groups elaborated and formalized the simple acts of preparing and administering black drink into rituals in their own right. Often specially designated individuals were assigned the task of brewing and then serving black drink in a carefully prescribed manner. The order in which they presented black drink to the individuals gathered for the occasion served as an index of the relative social status of the partakers; the most illustrious in the group received their portion of the decoction first, followed successively by individuals of decreasing status in the social hierarchy.

The impetus for elaborating the manner in which black drink was prepared, administered, and consumed derived at least in part from the fact that the significance of this decoction did not reside entirely in itself. For the southeastern Indians, black drink was a symbol, a vehicle for conveying and expressing a concept, a meaning. The principal referent of black drink was the concept of purity. Throughout the Southeast, black drink was invoked as a symbol of purity and employed in contexts where the expression and achievement of purity were of preeminent importance. The versatility of black drink as a symbol of purity was enhanced because it is a material substance and therefore readily manipulated. The southeastern Indians offered black drink to their former enemies during peacemaking ceremonies and presented the decoction or packets of *Ilex vomitoria* leaves to their visitors to indicate that their intentions were friendly and pure. Thus black drink served as a mediator and, in a sense, a lubricant of social relationships in the aboriginal Southeast.

The southeastern Indians' association between black drink and purity found its most dramatic expression in those contexts where they regurgitated it, but there is good reason to

believe that the connection between black drink and vomiting
was a symbolic rather than causal one. The emetic effect attributed to black drink seems to have resulted only after its
users consumed enormous quantities of the beverage, which
they voluntarily or involuntarily regurgitated. Also there is
some indication that several Indian groups occasionally added
certain purgative ingredients to their black drink to induce
vomiting. In smaller and purer doses, black drink served as a
caffeinated beverage—sipped daily by men in relatively informal gatherings, in divination and conjuring ceremonies, or
during council meetings—and as a nonemetic medicinal to
prevent or alleviate kidney disorders or to calm the nerves.
The southeastern Indians may have employed this otherwise
nonemetic decoction to induce vomiting because they associated black drink with purity and viewed vomiting as a means
of implementing and indicating the achievement of a particular state of purity. By consuming and then regurgitating an
acknowledged purifying agent, purification was doubly as-
sured.

The widespread consumption of black drink by the southeastern Indians appears to have declined considerably by the
late nineteenth century. By this time the southeastern Indian
groups who traditionally employed black drink had been either
destroyed or relocated in Oklahoma. In addition, the systems
established for the procurement of *Ilex vomitoria* presumably
would have broken down as cultivated groves of the shrub
were abandoned and traditional trading networks dismantled.
This does not mean that *Ilex vomitoria* was totally unavailable
to the relocated southeastern groups since the plant appears in
the southeastern portions of Oklahoma, in the territory
designated for Choctaw settlement. But I have discovered no
unequivocal evidence that any of the southeastern groups continued to prepare black drink for very long after their removal
from the Southeast. The introduction and availability of commercial caffeinated beverages such as coffee and tea no doubt
undermined the popularity of black drink. But perhaps a more
crucial factor was the disruption and intensive acculturation of

the southeastern Indians, which eventually led to the elimina-
tion of many of the traditional contexts within which black
drink was used. Since the use of black drink derived its raison
d'être and much of its significance from these contexts, a decline in its importance would be expected to have accompanied
the waning of the traditional southeastern Indian way of life.

NOTES

1. David Taitt, "Journal of David Taitt's Travels from Pensacola,
West Florida, to and through the Country of the Upper and Lower
Creeks, 1772," in *Travels in the American Colonies,* ed. Newton D.
Mereness (New York: Macmillan, 1916), pp. 556, 559; Louis Le Clerc
Milfort, *Memoirs or A Quick Glance at My Various Travels and My
Sojourn in the Creek Nation,* ed. and trans. Ben C. McCary (Kenne-
saw, Ga.: Continental Book Co., 1959), pp. 139–41; William Bartram,
*Travels through North and South Carolina, Georgia, East and West
Florida, the Cherokee Country, the Extensive Territories of the
Muscogulges or Creek Confederacy, and the Country of the Choctaws,*
2d ed. (London: no imprint, 1792), pp. 507–8. For an excellent edited
treatment of Bartram's travel journal, see William Bartram, *The
Travels of William Bartram,* ed. Francis Harper (New Haven: Yale
University Press, 1958).
2. The following discussion of Jonathan Dickinson's observations
on the use of black drink by the East Florida groups is based on
Jonathan Dickinson's Journal or, God's Protecting Providence, ed.
Evangeline W. Andrews and Charles M. Andrews (Philadelphia:
Reinier Jansen, 1945).
3. John R. Swanton, *Early History of the Creek Indians and Their
Neighbors,* Smithsonian Institution, Bureau of American Ethnology
Bulletin no. 73 (Washington, D.C., 1922), pp. 389–90. John M. Goggin and William C. Sturtevant separate the Jeaga and Jobé into two
distinct groups; see "The Calusa: A Stratified, Nonagricultural So-
ciety (With Notes on Sibling Marriage)," in *Explorations in Cultural
Anthropology: Essays in Honor of George Peter Murdock,* ed. Ward
H. Goodenough (New York: McGraw-Hill, 1964), fig. 1.
4. Swanton, *Early History,* p. 390; Do. d'Escalante Fontaneda,
*Memoir of Do. d'Escalante Fontaneda Respecting Florida, Written
in Spain, about the Year 1575,* ed. David O. True, trans. Buckingham
Smith (Coral Gables, Fla.: Glade House, 1945) (pp. 66–77 are a transcript of the original Spanish text).
5. Dickinson, *Journal,* pp. 45–47.

6. Ibid., p. 48. Laudonnière mentions that he received baskets of cassina leaves as a gift from the widow of a Timucuan chief somewhat to the north of the Ais. See Réné Goulaine de Laudonnière, in Jacques Le Moyne, *Narrative of Le Moyne, An Artist Who Accompanied the French Expedition to Florida under Laudonnière, 1564* (Boston: James R. Osgood and Co., 1875), p. 12.

7. Dickinson, *Journal*, pp. 56, 59–61.

8. Le Moyne, *Narrative*, pp. 16–23.

9. Ibid., "Descriptions of Illustrations," pp. 11–12.

10. Francisco Pareja, *Cathecismo, y Examen para los que Comulgan, en Lengua Castellana, y Timuquana* . . . (Mexico: Imprenta de Iuan Ruyz, 1627), p. 18r; idem, *Confessionario en Lengua Castellana, y Timuquana* . . . (Mexico: Imprenta de la Vivda de Diego Lopez Davalos, 1613), pp. 202r, 204r. Quotations supplied by Jerald T. Milanich.

11. Emile Perrot, *Matières Premières Usuelles du Règne Végétal. Thérapeutique–Hygiène–Industrie*, 2 vols. (Paris: Masson et Cie, Éditeurs Librairies de L'Académie de Médicine, 1943–1944), 2: 1340; Le Page du Pratz, *Histoire de la Louisiane* . . ., 3 vols. (Paris: De Bure, 1758), 2: 424–25; P. de Charlevoix, *Journal of a Voyage to North America* . . ., 2 vols. (London: Printed for R. and J. Dodsley, in Pall-Mall, 1761), 2: 305–6. Charlevoix calls it *Apalachina*.

12. Juan de Paina, "Origen y Principio del Juego de Pelota que los Indios Apalachinos y Ustacanos an estado jugando, Desde sus Infidelidad," manuscript of 1677, quoted and translated in *Some Considerations of the Apalachee Indians Based on the Paina Manuscript*, unpublished manuscript by John M. Goggin, Julian Granberry, and William C. Sturtevant, pp. 39–40. Manuscript in Sturtevant's possession.

13. Ibid., pp. 29–31.

14. Ibid., pp. 32–33.

15. We find a similar practice being observed by several groups living along the Gulf coast, as described by Cabeça de Vaca in the early sixteenth century. These groups kept their black drink pots covered to prevent pollution by any passing females. See Alvar Nuñez Cabeça de Vaca, *Relation of Alvar Nuñez Cabeça de Vaca*, trans. Buckingham Smith (New York: no imprint., 1871), p. 138.

16. William C. Sturtevant, "The Medicine Bundles and Busks of the Florida Seminole," *Florida Anthropologist* 7 (1954): 52–55. The Seminoles' use of ceremonial beverages is discussed more fully in Charles Fairbanks's chapter in this volume.

17. Swanton, *Early History*, p. 41.

18. Petrus Martyr de Angleria, *Opera: Legatio Babylonica, De Orbe Novo Decades Octo, Opus Epistolarum,* introduction by Erich Woldan (Graz, Austria: Akademische Druck- u. Verlagsanstalt, 1966),

pp. 218–20 (contains a facsimile of the 1st edition, 1530, of *De Orbe Novo Decades Octo*); translated in Peter Martyr D'Anghera, *De Orbo Novo: The Eight Decades of Peter Martyr D'Anghera*, ed. Francis A. MacNutt, 2 vols. (New York and London: G. P. Putnam's Sons, 1912), 2: 256–58, 266. MacNutt spells the name of this plant "Guihi," a difference resulting perhaps from his use of the later 1587 edition of *De Orbe Novo Decades Octo* as the basis for his translation (Martyr D'Anghera, *De Orbe Novo*, 2: 266).

19. Swanton, *Early History*, p. 45n4.

20. Fray Andrés de San Miguel, "Relación de los Trabajos que la Gente de vno Nao Llamada Nra. Señora de la Merced Padecio y Algunas Cosas Que en Aquella Flota Sucedieron," in *Dos Antiguas Relaciones de la Florida*, ed. Genaro García (Mexico: J. Aguilar Vera y Comp., 1902), pp. 196–97. Translated by John R. Swanton (*The Indians of the Southeastern United States*, Smithsonian Institution, Bureau of American Ethnology Bulletin no. 137 [Washington, D.C., 1946], pp. 791–92). Charlevoix mentions that the Indians mixed seawater with a decoction of *Ilex vomitoria* when they wanted a purge (Charlevoix, *Journal*, 2: 306).

21. Fray Pedro Muñoz, "Abstract of His History of Florida Missions, Presented to the Governor of St. Augustine, Oct. 5, 1722, by Priests of the Franciscan Convent," A.G.I., 58-1-29/42, pp. 102–6, Stetson Collection, Florida Ethnohistorical Survey, University of Florida Library. Translation supplied by Jerald T. Milanich.

22. William Byrd, *William Byrd's Histories of the Dividing Line Betwixt Virginia and North Carolina*, ed. William K. Boyd (Raleigh: North Carolina Historical Commission, 1929), p. 42; John Lawson, *A New Voyage to Carolina*, ed. Hugh T. Lefler (Chapel Hill: University of North Carolina Press, 1967), pp. 97–98.

23. Lawson establishes his three types of yaupon on the basis of variations in leaf size, leaf color, total plant size, and habitat. From his description of the three types, it appears that all three refer to the single taxonomic concept *Ilex vomitoria*.

24. Lawson, *A New Voyage*, pp. 97–98.

25. Ibid., pp. 229–30.

26. John Brickell, *The Natural History of North Carolina* (Raleigh: Trustees of the Public Libraries, 1911), pp. 39, 59, 87–88, 319, 323, 335, 342–43, 377, 399–400.

27. Mark Catesby, *The Natural History of Carolina, Florida and the Bahama Islands . . .*, 2 vols. (London: no imprint, 1731 and 1743), 2: 57.

28. Moses A. Curtis, "The Trees of North Carolina," in *The Woods and Timbers of North Carolina*, ed. Peter M. Hale (Raleigh: P. M. Hale; New York: E. J. Hale and Son, 1883), p. 99. It is impossible to determine exactly which groups are being discussed in

Curtis's passage. He places the description in quotes but does not give any reference to its author; I have been unable to locate the original source of this account. It could refer to any of the many groups in the Southeast who drank black drink, but since Curtis quotes it in his description of "The Trees of North Carolina," I have included it in the discussion of the use of black drink by the Carolina Indians.

29. To my knowledge, only Frank G. Speck has attempted to attribute the use of black drink to a specific Indian group from this area ("The Ethnic Position of the Southeastern Algonkian," *American Anthropologist* 26 [1924]: 193). Speck interprets drawings by John White of a group of Indians sitting around a fire or of several individuals dancing around a circle of posts as depicting a Secotan corn festival with strong indications of Muskogean influences, including the use of black drink. However, in my opinion, none of White's illustrations can be interpreted as depicting either a green corn ceremony or the use of black drink. For a reproduction of the illustrations in question and additional comments by William C. Sturtevant on Speck's interpretation of them, see Paul Hulton and David B. Quinn, eds., *The American Drawings of John White 1577–1590 . . .*, 2 vols. (London: Trustees of the British Museum; Chapel Hill: University of North Carolina Press, 1964), 1: 95–100, 2: pls. 31, 35, 38, 39.

30. Frank G. Speck, "Remnants of the Machapunga Indians of North Carolina," *American Anthropologist* 18 (1916): 273.

31. I was pleased to discover that yaupon tea is available on the menu of the Pony Island Restaurant on Ocracoke Island, North Carolina. In 1973 a small package of prepared leaves could be purchased at the restaurant for fifty cents.

32. Frank G. Speck, *Catawba Medicines and Curative Practices,* Publications of the Philadelphia Anthropological Society, Twenty-fifth Anniversary Studies, vol. 1 (1937), pp. 189, 195n23, 195–97n24.

33. For a discussion of some of the emesis-inducing plants and ceremonial decoctions employed by the Virginia Algonquians, see William L. Merrill and Christian F. Feest, "An Exchange of Botanical Information in the Early Contact Situation: *Wisakon* of the Southeastern Algonquians," *Economic Botany* 29 (1975): 171–84.

34. Several writers discuss the wide range of plants employed by the Cherokees to achieve purification, none of which can with any certainty be identified as *Ilex vomitoria*. See John Witthoft, "The Cherokee Green Corn Medicine and the Green Corn Festival," *Journal of the Washington Academy of Sciences* 36 (1946): 213n2, 215; idem, *Green Corn Ceremonialism in the Eastern Woodlands,* Occasional Contributions from the Museum of Anthropology of the University of Michigan, vol. 13 (1949), pp. 44–47; James Mooney and

Frans M. Olbrechts, *The Swimmer Manuscript: Cherokee Sacred Formulas and Medicinal Prescriptions,* Smithsonian Institution, Bureau of American Ethnology Bulletin no. 99 (Washington, D.C., 1932), passim; Raymond D. Fogelson, "The Cherokee Ballgame: A Study in Southeastern Ethnology" (Ph.D. diss., University of Pennsylvania, 1962), pp. 72–73, 248–57; Alexander Longe, "A Small Postscript on the Ways and Manners of the Indians Called Cherokees . . .," ed. David H. Corkran, *Southern Indian Studies* 21 (1969): 16–17, 44–47; and Henry Timberlake, *The Memoirs of Lieut. Henry Timberlake* (London: no imprint, 1765), pp. 77–79.

35. William C. Sturtevant, personal communication, 1973; Duane H. King, personal communication, 1973.

36. Bartram, *Travels,* p. 357.

37. John P. Brown, *Old Frontiers: The Story of the Cherokee Indians from Earliest Times to the Date of their Removal to the West, 1838* (Kingsport, Tenn.: Southern Publishers, 1938), pp. 148–49.

38. Bartram, *Travels,* p. 357.

39. Swanton believes the Yuchis were relative latecomers to the Southeast. For his discussion of this question, see Swanton, *Early History,* pp. 286–312.

40. Christian Hvidt, *Von Reck's Voyage to Georgia in 1736* (Savannah, Ga.: The Beehive Press, in press).

41. Frank G. Speck, *Ethnology of the Yuchi Indians,* Anthropological Publications of the University Museum, University of Pennsylvania, vol. 1, no. 1 (1909), pp. 106–36.

42. Jean-Bernard Bossu, *Nouveaux Voyages aux Indes Occidentales,* 2 vols. (Paris: no imprint, 1768), 2: 41–42 (my translation). Baron Marc de Villiers ("Documents Concernant l'Historie des Indiens de la Region Orientale de la Louisiane," *Journal de la Société des Américanistes de Paris,* n.s., 14 [1922]: 136) reproduces a sketch of an eighteenth-century Alabama squareground cabin (see fig. 12) depicting, among other things, three conch shells arranged on the floor of the cabin. Perhaps the Alabamas served black drink from these shell cups in a manner similar to the one described here by Bossu.

43. Bossu, *Nouveaux Voyages,* 2: 43–46.

44. Jean-Bernard Bossu, *Jean-Bernard Bossu's Travels in the Interior of North America,* ed. and trans. Seymour Feiler (Norman: University of Oklahoma Press, 1962), p. 196.

45. John R. Swanton, *Religious Beliefs and Medical Practices of the Creek Indians,* Smithsonian Institution, Bureau of American Ethnology Annual Report no. 42 (1928), p. 666.

46. James Adair, *The History of the American Indians* (London: no imprint, 1775), p. 165. Among the Creeks, the *Yahola* cry, uttered

while black drink was being taken, was intended to imitate the cry of *Yahola*, an important male deity noted for his perfect purity (Swanton, *Religious Beliefs*, p. 485).

47. Adair, *History*, p. 361.

48. Ibid., pp. 108, 160–68.

49. Ibid., pp. 99–111; Witthoft, *Green Corn Ceremonialism*, p. 53.

50. Frank G. Speck, "Notes on Chickasaw Ethnology and Folk-Lore," *Journal of American Folk-Lore* 20 (1907): 56.

51. John R. Swanton, *Social and Religious Beliefs and Usages of the Chickasaw Indians*, Smithsonian Institution, Bureau of American Ethnology Annual Report no. 44 (1928), p. 262; idem, *Religious Beliefs*, p. 590.

52. Victor Tixier, *Tixier's "Travels on the Osage Prairies,"* ed. John F. McDermott, trans. Albert J. Salvan (Norman: University of Oklahoma Press, 1940), p. 81.

53. Albert S. Gatschet relates that Chitimacha shamans drank and smoked "cassine" to induce a stupor in which they divined the future ("Texts of the Shetimasha Language, spoken in Charenton, St. Mary's Parish, La.," Smithsonian Institution, National Anthropological Archives, ms. 288-a).

54. David I. Bushnell, Jr., *The Choctaw of Bayou Lacomb, St. Tammany Parish, Louisiana*, Smithsonian Institution, Bureau of American Ethnology Bulletin no. 48 (Washington, D.C., 1909), p. 10.

55. David I. Bushnell, Jr., "Some New Ethnologic Data from Louisiana," *Journal of the Washington Academy of Sciences* 12 (1922): 304.

56. Bernard Romans, *A Concise History of East and West Florida*, a facsimile reproduction of the 1775 edition (Gainesville: University of Florida Press, 1962), pp. 85–86.

57. Bartram, *Travels*, p. 357; Lawson, *A New Voyage*, pp. 97–98.

58. Albert S. Gatschet, "Shetimasha; Words & Sentences collected Dec. '81 & Jan. '82 . . . ; To accompany Texts of Same Language," Smithsonian Institution, National Anthropological Archives, ms. 349-a; Gatschet, "Texts of the Shetimasha Language."

59. Albert S. Gatschet, "The Shetimasha Indians of St. Mary's Parish, Southern Louisiana," *Transactions of the Anthropological Society of Washington* 2 (1883): 156–57.

60. John R. Swanton, *Indian Tribes of the Lower Mississippi Valley and Adjacent Coast of the Gulf of Mexico*, Smithsonian Institution, Bureau of American Ethnology Bulletin no. 43 (Washington, D.C., 1911), p. 351; idem, "Chitimacha-English Dictionary, utilizing Chitimacha-English dictionary of A. S. Gatschet, with revisions based on field work in Charenton, La., 1908–1931," Smithsonian Institution, National Anthropological Archives, ms. 2439, box 1.

61. Le Page du Pratz, *Histoire de la Louisiane . . .*, 2: 424–25.

Translated by Swanton, *Indian Tribes of the Lower Mississippi*, pp. 130–31. Le Page du Pratz states that this drink was intoxicating (*enyvre*).

62. Charlevoix, *Journal*, 2: 303.

63. [Mathurin] le Petit, "Lettre du Père le Petit, Missionnaire, au Père d'Anvugour, Procureur des Missions de l'Amérique Septentrionale. À la Nouvelle Orléans, le 12 Juillet, 1730," in *The Jesuit Relations and Allied Documents: Travels and Explorations of the Jesuit Missionaries in New France, 1610–1791*, ed. Reuben G. Thwaites, 73 vols. (Cleveland: Burrows Brothers Co., 1896–1901), 68: 145.

64. Taitt, "Journal," in Mereness, *Travels*, pp. 531–32.

65. Paul du Ru, *Journal of Paul du Ru*, trans. Ruth L. Butler (Chicago: Caxton Club, 1934), pp. 28–29.

66. Frank G. Speck, "A List of Plant Curatives Obtained from the Houma Indians of Louisiana," *Primitive Man* 14 (1941): 49–73.

67. Cabeça de Vaca, *Relation*, pp. 137–38.

68. This cry may have been comparable to the *Yahola* cry of the Creeks and possibly other southeastern groups. Specially designated persons sang out this cry while the other participants in the ceremony partook of black drink. In some instances the drinker had to imbibe black drink throughout the duration of the yell.

69. Cabeça de Vaca, *Relation*, pp. 137–38, 139n3.

70. John R. Swanton, *Source Material on the History and Ethnology of the Caddo Indians*, Smithsonian Institution, Bureau of American Ethnology Bulletin no. 132 (Washington, D.C., 1942), p. 29.

71. Henri Folmer, "De Bellisle on the Texas Coast," *Southwestern Historical Quarterly* 44 (1940): 216–17.

72. Bossu, *Nouveaux Voyages*, 2: 140n1.

73. J. O. Dyer, *The Lake Charles Atakapas (Cannibals) Period of 1817 to 1820* (Galveston: no imprint, 1917), [p. 4].

74. Alice W. Oliver, "Notes on the Carancahua Indians," in *The Karankawa Indians*, ed. Albert S. Gatschet, Papers of the Peabody Museum of American Archaeology and Ethnology, vol. 1, no. 2 (1891), pp. 18–19.

75. The best study of the early history and culture of the Caddo is John R. Swanton's *Source Material on the History and Ethnology of the Caddo Indians*. For information on the modern Caddo, see Elsie C. Parsons, *Notes on the Caddo*, American Anthropological Association Memoir no. 57 (1941), pp. 1–76.

76. Fray Isidro Felis de Espinosa, "Fray Isidro Felis de Espinosa on the Asinai and their Allies," in "Descriptions of the Tejas or Asinai Indians, 1691–1722," ed. and trans. Mattie A. Hatcher, *Southwestern Historical Quarterly* 31 (1927–1928): 171–74.

77. Fray Juan Agustín de Morfi, *Excerpts from the Memorias for the History of the Province of Texas*, ed. and trans. Frederick C.

Chabot, rev. trans. by Carlos E. Castaneda (San Antonio: privately published, 1932), p. 31; Fray Francisco Hidalgo, "Fray Francisco Hidalgo to Fray Isidro Cassos, November 20, 1710 (Extract); Fray Francisco Hidalgo to the Viceroy, November 4, 1716," in "Descriptions of the Tejas or Asinai Indians, 1691–1722," ed. and trans. Mattie A. Hatcher, *Southwestern Historical Quarterly* 31 (1927–1928): 52.

78. Morfi, *Memorias*, p. 35.

79. Espinosa, "Asinai," in Hatcher, "Tejas," p. 168.

80. Jean Louis Berlandier, "Les moeurs et coutumes des Indigènes nomades des Etats Internes d'Orient et d'Occident des territoires du Nouveau Mexique et des deux Californes," ms. in Thomas Gilcrease Institute of American History and Art, Tulsa, Oklahoma, photocopy in the possession of John C. Ewers, p. 111r; idem, *The Indians of Texas in 1830*, ed. John C. Ewers, trans. Patricia Reading Leclercq (Washington, D.C.: Smithsonian Institution Press, 1969), p. 89. After the publication of Ewers's edition of this Berlandier manuscript, William C. Sturtevant discovered Berlandier's specimens of *Ilex vomitoria* in the New York Botanical Garden and the Gray Herbarium and Arnold Arboretum of Harvard University, collector's no. 1811 (William C. Sturtevant, personal communication, 1972).

81. Berlandier, *Indians of Texas*, p. 147. Gustav G. Carlson and Volney H. Jones mention that the Comanche prepared a tea from the leaves of a plant whose description they feel suggests *Ilex vomitoria;* however, they were unable to establish a definite identification of this plant ("Some Notes on the Uses of Plants by the Comanche Indians," *Papers of the Michigan Academy of Science, Arts and Letters* 25 [1939]: 531–32).

Origins and Prehistoric Distributions of Black Drink and the Ceremonial Shell Drinking Cup

Jerald T. Milanich

We know from historic accounts that black drink was usually drunk from a shell dipper or cup. Many European accounts of the sixteenth, seventeenth, and eighteenth centuries describe such ceremonies, and drawings by the Frenchman Jacque Le Moyne show the Timucua Indians of eastern Florida drinking black drink from a shell cup (see fig. 4). Both black drink and the shell drinking cup had religious significance, and the two were intimately associated in the ceremonial life of the southeastern Indians.

The prehistoric usage of the drink has previously been investigated in studies of the Southern Cult (also called the Southeastern Ceremonial Complex), an archaeological complex of certain objects and symbols widespread among southeastern horticulturalists by about A.D. 1200. The Southern Cult paraphernalia and art styles seem to have been associated with certain important individuals and had religious as well as political and social significance. Cult objects were often placed in the graves—some as part of a costume—of such high status individuals, who were often interred within or adjacent to temples or other ceremonial structures. Shell drinking cups engraved with cult symbols are common at the large prehistoric ceremonial centers associated with the cult, and in two instances, residues, thought to be from evaporated black drink, have been found in shell cups at such centers. The use of the cups and black drink was an important part of the religion of

Part of the research and preparation of this paper was carried out while the author was supported by a National Endowment for the Humanities postdoctoral fellowship at the Smithsonian Institution.

the late prehistoric southeastern aborigines, a pattern that was still in practice four hundred years later at the time of European contact.

The widespread distribution of the cups, which has been substantiated by historical and archaeological evidence, may indicate that the origins of black drink date back earlier than the Southern Cult. By the time of the cult, both a drink ritual and shell cups were evidently widely distributed in the Southeast; but that such a drink was brewed from *Ilex vomitoria* is not certain. Archaeological evidence suggests that some type of drink was a part of Hopewellian ceremonialism, which was distributed throughout the Southeast for several centuries after A.D. 1. Although such evidence is very tenuous, it does demonstrate that the use of shell drinking cups has a long history in the Southeast, extending back into the pre-Hopewellian Archaic cultures. Formalization of the taking of the drink as part of a religious ceremony may have also occurred over a long period prior to the appearance of Mississippian ceremonialism. There is also speculation that Mesoamerican religious-horticultural beliefs played a role in the formation of the black drink ceremonials, but the evidence is not conclusive.[1]

Although it is not possible for the archaeologist actually to excavate the behavior connected with the black drink ceremonies, a great deal can be learned about its origins, distribution, and significance by studying the various cultural and ritual contexts in which shell cups are found. Shell, except in extremely acidic soils, lasts for thousands of years. Archaeologists have recovered shells that may have been black drink containers, and, on occasion, fire hearths or burials have been found in association with the cups. By interpreting the relationships between these features and artifacts, inferences can be made about the behavior patterns associated with their deposition. In several instances, carefully controlled excavations have revealed what seem to be locations where black drink was used. However, only when the cups are found in contexts that resemble those described in ethnohistorical or ethnological documents can we strongly postulate that the cups and the black drink were present together. Such contexts include: (1) shell cups as grave goods with burials in grave pits, tombs, or burial mounds; (2) shell cups in burial mounds as separate deposits (see figs. 5 and 6); (3) shell cups in burial mounds along with other items, usually mortuary pottery, as special caches; (4) shell cups on living floors of ceremonial structures, such as earthlodges, rotundas, or temples, in which historically the drink was known to have been drunk; and (5) shell cups with other vessels or with fire hearths whose location, such as a mound surface or structure's living floor, suggests the use or the brewing of the drink.

SPECIES OF SHELLS USED AS CUPS

Although nine species of marine shells shaped into cups have been reported in the literature from archaeological sites in the eastern United States, a recent analysis of many of these cups indicates that many early investigators incorrectly identified a number of the shells. In actuality, only three species have been confirmed as having been made into cups: lightning whelk, emperor helmet, and horse conch.[2]

Making a cup from any one of these shells was a relatively simple process. The center columella, which runs longitudinally down the shell, was removed by cutting along its length. This left a long dipperlike cup, whose cut edges and original shell lip were ground down and polished to form the finished product.

Of the three shells, the species with by far the widest distribution, and the one used most frequently as a cup, is the *Busycon contrarium* Conrad (lightning whelk), which is found along the coast from Cape Hatteras, North Carolina, south to Cuba and around the Gulf coast to Louisiana. It is most common along the Florida Gulf coast, occurring in the largest quantities off the coast of Lee County, Florida. The largest of the *Busycon* shell species, *B. contrarium,* occasionally attains a length of sixteen inches. Because of its left-handed spiral, the lightning whelk is frequently confused with *Busycon perversum* Linné, the perverse whelk that also spirals to the left. This latter species, however, never reaches the length of *B. contrarium*. It is found along the eastern coast of Mexico from Campeche Bay northward and around the Gulf to Louisiana. *B. contrarium* and *B. perversum* may be geographical variants.

The way in which the shells spiral may have been an important factor in their selection for use as cups. Among southeastern aborigines the spiral was both an art motif and a pattern used in dance and ritual; a left-handed spiral may have had a significance different from that of a right-handed spiral. The spiral is a Mesoamerican symbol which may have been introduced to the United States. Thus, the lightning whelk may have been used as a drinking cup because of its spiral as well as because of its size and availability.

Another species of shell occasionally used as a cup is the emperor helmet, *Cassis madagascarensis* Lamarck, which is distributed from southeastern Florida through the Keys into the Bahamas. Used even less frequently is the horse conch, *Pleuroploca gigantea* Kiener, found on both coasts of Florida southward through the Keys.

The species of several shell drinking cups found at noncoastal sites have been identified incorrectly. These include: *B. perversum, B. carica, B. spiratum, Cassis tuberosa, Fasciolaria tulipa,* and *Melongena corona.* Although these shells may have been traded inland for other uses, positive identification of their use as cups still needs to be made.

Artifacts made from species of marine shells have been found at prehistoric sites as far west as Oklahoma and as far north as Wisconsin. Shell, an exotic raw material to noncoastal peoples, was traded extensively. During the period between 200 B.C. and A.D. 1000 the most advanced or complex cultures in the Southeast were in west and northwest Florida, southwest Georgia, and in the lower Mississippi River Valley. It is likely that the largest number of shells were traded inland through these areas, even though these shells might originally have been obtained from the Florida coasts. Copper, exotic stone, pottery vessels, and other northern goods have been found at a number of sites in the Gulf region (e.g., Mandeville in southwest Georgia and Crystal River and Yent on the Florida coast), and trade between these cultures and other cultures to the north, including those of the Ohio and Tennessee river drainage areas, has been well documented.[3]

ARCHAIC PERIOD—6,000 B.C. TO 200 B.C.

The interior hunting and gathering cultures of the southeastern United States traded for marine shell and used it in making many types of decorative artifacts. In the Archaic period, however, shell cups seem to have been used only infrequently; examples have been found as grave goods with burials of a very few individuals.

At the Carlson Annis shell midden site in Butler County, Kentucky, a typical Archaic river valley site, shell cups were present with only two out of 390 burials—one an infant and the other an adolescent.[4] Two large shell cups had been placed on the infant burial, both cups having perforations in their narrow ends. The practice of drilling holes through the narrow ends of the cups was widespread, beginning early and continuing into the Mississippian period, after A.D. 1000. The purpose of the holes is unknown—perhaps they were used to attach a thong for suspending the cups. The Carlson Annis site is radiocarbon dated between 5000 B.C. and 2000 B.C.

The Indian Knoll site, another Archaic site in west-central Kentucky, was occupied from 3000 B.C. to 1000 B.C. and also contained shell cups with burials.[5] At the site, 275 burials (31.4 percent of the total number of burials at the site) contained grave goods, but only five of these were accompanied by shell cups. The five burials, showing no pattern with respect to sex and age, consist of: one adult male, one infant, one child (possibly female) about ten years of age, one adolescent about fifteen years of age, and one female about twenty-two years of age. With the exception of the child burial, relatively large amounts of other items had been placed in each grave. Two of the burials, adjacent to one another, were decorated with a total of 5,171 shell beads of various types, along with two bone awls, animal teeth, and shell pendants. At the Stalling's Island site in Columbia County, Georgia, on the Savannah River, one burial was found with a shell cup.[6] The Stalling's Island Archaic occupation dates from roughly the same period as Indian Knoll.

Data from these sites indicate a wide noncoastal distribution for the shell cups prior to 1000 B.C. Also, during this period, use of the shell cup as a grave item was not restricted to any one sex or age group. Probably these exotic shell vessels and the other shell artifacts were possessed by only a few families, who had acquired them along with other marine shell items through trade. Marine shell was a valued commodity probably because of its scarcity rather than because of its ceremonial or religious significance. There is no evidence of a black drink ceremonial during the Archaic period.

Shell cups have not been recovered from the Poverty Point site in Louisiana, even though the Poverty Point people must have practiced complex ceremonialism by 1000 B.C.[7] Nor do shell cups appear in the Ohio Valley Adena culture with its developed ceremonialism dating after 1000 B.C. Cups do appear in the middens of the lower Mississippi Valley Tchefuncte culture, which is roughly equivalent temporally to Adena.[8] These cups, however, seem not to have had religious significance or high status value, for they are found with other utilitarian objects in the refuse from everyday activities. We can conclude that during the Archaic period shell cups as valued items were restricted in distribution largely to the river valley regions of the southeastern highlands and piedmont where they were acquired by trade.

HOPEWELLIAN CEREMONIALISM—200 B.C. TO A.D. 500

Between 1000 B.C. and A.D. 1 horticulture became known in

the eastern United States, and the evidence points to southern Florida (Okeechobee Basin) and the midwestern United States as areas of early maize cultivation. The relationship between these two regions is only now being discovered, and it is not yet certain which area received knowledge of maize horticulture first.[9] This new source of food, added to indigenous subsistence patterns—including the intensive harvesting of wild food resources and the cultivation of a limited number of plants—may have been associated with the formation of the Hopewellian trade sphere throughout much of the eastern United States. Although the Hopewellian culture seems to have been centered in the states of Ohio, Illinois, Indiana, and Kentucky, Hopewellian ceremonial practices were present among many cultures from the Great Lakes to Florida.[10] Main elements of the complex are log tomb burials; an array of symbolic figures, earthworks, and artifacts; and nonegalitarian sociopolitical organization, perhaps with inherited chief-priest (head trader?) positions.

During the geographical spread of Hopewellian ceremonialism, the shell cup also became widespread, possibly taking on a significance beyond being simply a rare and valued drinking container, as had been the case among earlier Archaic cultures. Although the cup continued to be placed in burials, its association with other specialized grave goods—mortuary pottery, engraved stone and copper tablets, and other such items—indicates new symbolic significance for the cup. This change may mark the beginning of black drink ceremonialism or something similar to it.

With the increased trade in the eastern United States during the early Formative period, it is possible that *Ilex vomitoria*—known to possess certain desirable qualities by the aborigines in the Southeast, where the plant naturally occurred—became an item of trade to the interior. Because *I. vomitoria* and the shell cups were highly esteemed, and because both are found within the same coastal areas, the two may have been traded together. This link might well have led to the ceremonial association of shell cups and black drink in cultures away from the coast, where shell cups had long been prized items. It is tempting to hypothesize that these two items were traded to the peoples of the Tennessee River drainages in exchange for the exotic stone, pottery, and copper objects that show up in Florida and southwest Georgia during the Formative period. Thus, it is possible that with the evolution and spread of the Hopewellian complex, a ceremony involving the taking of black drink or other medicine from shell cups also spread and became a common trait among the prehistoric aborigines of the Southeast.

The distribution of shell cups as ceremonial items during the period of the Hopewellian complex ranged from the midwestern United States southward into Florida. James B. Griffin, writing more than twenty years ago, observed that *Busycon* and *Cassis* shells were quite common at midwestern Hopewell culture sites; in fact, he noted that "the *Cassis* shell is almost a time marker in the Hopewellian Horizon."[11] The cups, however, are not found in the village middens of the Hopewell people.[12] They were not items of everyday use; rather they were restricted to special cultural contexts, which are reflected in their archaeological contexts. For example, many cups are found in Hopewellian burial tombs, where they were usually placed beside the head of the corpse; often they are the only grave offering present.[13] This practice might have been similar to the historic Timuca Indians' custom of burying a chief's shell cup with him.

At the Wilson site, a Hopewell culture village in the Illinois Wabash Valley, a shell cup was found with other artifacts in a log tomb. In the tomb was a central burial surrounded by five other burials, possibly sacrificial offerings. The central burial was accompanied by a sandstone tubular pipe, cut mussel shells, limestone hemispheres, *Marginella* shell beads, and bone tools. Possibly the burial was that of the priest or priest-chief, some of whose ceremonial paraphernalia, including the cup, was placed in the tomb with him.[14] The individual awarded special burial status probably held high social importance in life, and the artifacts with him held significance because of

Figure 5. Burial of a Timucuan chief in a mound with his shell cup placed on the mound surface. From de Bry, *Florida*, pl. XL. Courtesy of the Smithsonian Institution, National Anthropological Archives, negative no. 57,580.

their association with his rank. They were not merely exotic trade items, as in the Archaic period.

An adult female burial at the same site was interred with a shell cup and a spoonlike shell artifact. Such spoonlike shell artifacts are common with Hopewellian complex burials and may have been ceremonial eating or drinking implements. Placement of the female burial suggests that she was sacrificed to accompany the central log tomb burial. This could indicate either that both males and females used shell cups or that perhaps before his death she had been the person who had served the cup and its contents to the individual interred in the log tomb.

Cups accompanying the corpses of what probably were high status individuals are found throughout the geographical range of the Hopewellian complex, and they are common in the tombs of the Ohio Hopewell culture and also in the tombs of the Hopewellian Marksville culture located along the Mississippi River from Baton Rouge north to Memphis.[15] An excellent example of their association with the Marksville culture is provided by James A. Ford's excavation in northeastern Arkansas of a mound containing eight group burials, five of which were in log tombs.[16] Of the eight, six had one or more shell cups accompanying them. The other two burial groups were accompanied by pottery vessels, and both had shell spoons. One pottery vessel had two holes drilled just below the rim, probably for suspension of the pot. Drilled vessels often occur with shell cups during the early Formative period and may have been used in a black drink ceremony. One adolescent burial tomb contained the following items: a three-tube copper panpipe covered with silver (found lying on the individual's chest); earspools (in each hand); shell beads (around the ankles, neck, wrists, and upper arms); and a belt of wolf teeth and shell beads. A shell cup had also been placed in the tomb. This important and youthful individual must have had prestige that was accorded to him on the basis of his birth rather than on the basis of any special skills or occupation. Perhaps he was the heir to the priest-chief position.

At the same site cups were found with the following burials: two adolescents; one child; one adult female; one adult of unknown sex; and with a group of two old adult females, one adult male, and a ten-year-old child, none of which seems to have been the central burial. In all cases the cups were placed open bowl up and could have contained liquid.

Shell cups are also common in the Hopewellian-related Copena burial complex in northeastern Alabama. In some instances the cups were placed upside down over the face of the corpse rather than beside the head.[17] The latter burial placement is more common, however.

Variations in the Hopewellian burial complex in Florida are evident at a number of sites, and possible evidence for black drink ceremonialism is also widely distributed in that state. Along the north Florida Gulf coast, William H. Sears has grouped artifacts associated with Hopewellian ceremonialism into two temporally successive burial complexes, the Yent and Green Point complexes.[18] The earlier Yent complex, dated from about 200 B.C. to A.D. 100 or later, is associated with burial mounds of the late Deptford and early Swift Creek cultures. Trade between these cultures and the midwest Hopewell cultures seems to have been common. In fact, many of the exotic Yent burial goods, especially the silver, copper, and stone ornaments and religious paraphernalia, may have been traded directly from northern Hopewellian sites in return for southern marine shells and *Ilex vomitoria*. By A.D. 100 or so, there was enough change in the Yent complex artifact inventory to warrant the defining of the Green Point complex. In west Florida, and possibly in southwest Georgia, the Green Point complex was associated with the Swift Creek culture. The Green Point Hopewellian complex seems to have retained its homogeneity until some time after A.D. 500, when it developed into Weeden Island ceremonialism.

Shell cups have been found with burials or in pottery deposits in many sites of the Yent complex. Frequently vessels made for special uses were placed with burials or in separate caches in the Yent burial mounds. These special mortuary

vessels, so-called because of their nonutilitarian nature and
their occurrence in burial mounds, were usually manufactured
in unusual shapes and sizes—often plant, animal, or human
effigies—and may have been intended for use in a black drink
ceremony along with the shell cups. At the Alligator Bayou
site in Bay County in west Florida, shell cups were excavated
with teacup-size miniature ceramic vessels, possibly drinking
containers for sacred medicines other than black drink.[19] In
Liberty County one shell cup was found by Clarence B. Moore
with forty-six other vessels in a mound mortuary cache.[20] All
of the vessels and the cup were symbolically "killed" by having
their bottoms knocked out. It is generally believed that this
practice was done in an effort to release the spirit of the vessel
to allow it to accompany the deceased to a life after death.

The exact nature of the ritual associated with the killing of
pots and the deposition of large numbers of these pots in burial
mounds is unknown. More often than not in the Yent deposits
a shell cup is present. An alternative explanation to the popular "spirit-freeing" hypothesis is that the vessels were used in a
black drink or similar ceremony by the priests and then killed
to prevent use by nonsanctified individuals. This would explain the presence of shell cups within the deposits.

Another explanation is that the vessels accidentally broken
at various ceremonies were saved until they could be buried in
a ritually prepared mound deposit. Again, their deposition
would have been to prevent nonsanctified individuals from
using the vessels. The deposition of intentionally and/or accidentally destroyed vessels might have been at certain times of
the year when burials that had been cleaned and stored in
charnel houses could also be interred in the mounds especially
prepared for them. In the Southeast there is historic evidence
for special handling of holy or sacred paraphernalia to prevent
contact with nonsanctified persons or objects. There is also
evidence from Mississippian sites after A.D. 1000 in the Southeast that religious structures such as mounds, temples, council
houses, and charnel houses were periodically torn down and
rebuilt. The reuse of mounds for the interment of burials and

religious vessels might have been related to such a practice. Perhaps this pattern had a long history in the eastern United States. Two other Yent burial mounds where shell cups have been found are the Yent mound in Franklin County, Florida, and the Crystal River site in Citrus County, Florida.[21] In the Yent mound a shell cup was found on top of a skull burial along with mortuary ceramic vessels. One clay vessel was in the shape of a *Busycon* shell whorl, suggesting that the ceramic mortuary pots were used for functions similar to those of the shell cups and that the spirals had special significance.[22] At the Crystal River site, fifty-three shell drinking cups were taken from the large burial mound. The cups were accompanied by a large assortment of exotic Hopewellian religious artifacts and full-sized and miniature mortuary vessels.

Perhaps the best evidence for a black drink ceremony, or something similar to it, associated with Yent burial ritual comes from Pierce Mound A in Franklin County, where shell cups were found with miniature vessels and mortuary pottery.[23] On the ground surface on which the mound was built, surrounding a hearth, excavators found scattered food bones, one wolf tooth, one puma tooth, and a shell cup. Possibly some sort of black drink ritual took place before construction of the mound began. Evidence for such a pre–mound construction ceremony becomes stronger during the post-Hopewellian religion period in Florida.

That the shell cup was used as a special vessel in the Yent burial ceremonialism is evident from these archaeological contexts. The cups have been found associated with small ceramic vessels (usually cylindrical cups or pots) and with mortuary vessels that were made in nonutilitarian shapes and sizes, all of which may have been involved in the black drink ritual and in the drinking of other ceremonial medicines. It therefore seems likely that during the Formative period in Florida, various cultures used some kind of drink in a pre-mound purification ceremony, perhaps purification of the persons who were involved in the actual construction of the mound. A drink seems to have been used in other ceremonies away from the

Figure 6. Burial of Timucuan warriors in a mound with weapons and shell cups as grave goods. From de Bry, *Florida*, Plate 19. [...]

mound; periodically, used or broken shell cups and other paraphernalia used in the drink ritual may have been deposited in
a mound to prevent their use by and contact with nonsanctified persons. Occasionally shell cups were also placed with
human burials.

Uses of the shell cup in the later Green Point complex were
little changed from those of the Yent complex, although killing of the cups seems to have been more common. Some of the
Green Point mortuary pottery continued to have perforations
(for suspension) under the rim.[24] The overall spatial distribution of Green Point shell cups is greater than for those of Yent,
perhaps reflecting the spread of the complex and an increased
use of the drink. At least ten sites containing the shell cups
and dating from the period of the Green Point complex were
excavated by C. B. Moore along the Florida Gulf coast from
the Alabama border to Crystal River.[25]

POSSIBLE MESOAMERICAN INFLUENCES ON THE EASTERN UNITED STATES SYMBOLISM

Scholars of the prehistoric period agree that the introduction
of maize horticulture into the United States was a result of contact with Mesoamerican peoples. The exact nature and in-
tensity of this contact in the eastern United States is still
debated. The fact that only one or two pieces of pottery
thought to be from Mesoamerica have been found at southeastern sites suggests that this contact was not by migrations of
groups of peoples, as in colonizing expeditions. Some archaeologists have hypothesized that knowledge of maize could
come from occasional contact with traders or missionaries along
established routes overland through Texas and Oklahoma, or
perhaps by sea across the Gulf of Mexico. Maize horticulture
might also have been first introduced into the Midwest from
the southwestern United States, not from Mexico.

Certain southeastern art motifs and ceramic styles of the
Hopewellian complex (and later, the Mississippian symbolism)

do seem related to Mesoamerican styles. It is possible that along with maize, certain religious beliefs and practices associated with horticulture were also diffused to the early southeastern cultures. These concepts could have been incorporated in slightly altered form into the Hopewellian complex, which formed the basis for later southeastern religious developments.

David S. Phelps has pointed out that certain Mayan Indian glyphs from Mesoamerica resemble Hopewellian and Mississippian period decorations found on southeastern clay pots and shell and copper ornaments.[26] Although many archaeologists have noted similarities between specific southeastern and Mesoamerican ceramic traits, thus suggesting some sort of contact, Phelps has begun a study of specific glyph meanings and their forms of occurrence.[27] His preliminary study concludes that southeastern religious symbolism is "a duplicate of that in Mesoamerica proper. . . . and can only be understood when explained in terms of the ideological source."[28]

Phelps's work is relevant to this study of the black drink ceremony, since several glyph elements thought to have been introduced to the Southeast from Mesoamerica, relate to marine conch shells—the spiral design, the conch shell, the shell section, and the abstract shell design—and to the symbolic giving of water and sacred fluids by the gods, symbolized by an inverted hand (see fig. 7). These glyph elements have been placed by J. E. S. Thompson into two major groupings—Water and Underworld—which are both associated in Mesoamerican belief systems with horticultural fertility.[29] It is possible that these symbols and their associated meanings were brought to the Southeast as a part of the Mesoamerican maize horticultural complex. They are widely distributed in time and space in the Southeast, and the attachment of religious significance to the shell cup and the linking of black drink (a sacred fluid) to the cup may have been originally the result of Mesoamerican influences on indigenous Southeast practices. A great deal of research, however, is needed to describe more clearly the symbolic aspects of the general Southeast belief system and to demonstrate specific ties with Mesoamerica.

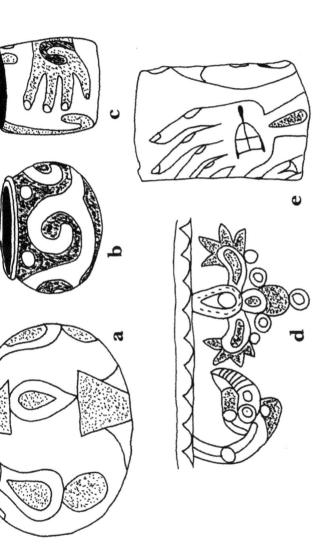

Figure 7. Mesoamerican glyphs and glyph elements on southeastern pottery. **a.** Crystal River Incised vessel with teardrop-shaped abstract shell glyph elements. **b.** Crystal River Negative Painted vessel with spiral shell glyph elements. **c.** Crystal River Zoned Red vessel with inverted hand glyph element. **d.** Crystal River Incised vessel with conch shell glyph. **e.** Crystal River Incised pot fragment with hand and abstract shell glyph elements. (**d,** from Moore, "Northwest Florida Coast," fig. 158; the others from Moore, "Florida Central-West Coast," figs. 21, 27, 148–149, 18.)

POST-HOPEWELLIAN CEREMONIALISM—
A.D. 500 TO A.D. 1000

The decline of the Hopewellian trade network and the disappearance of the Hopewellian burial cult in the Southeast were followed by the development of regional ceremonial complexes. No doubt many of the Hopewellian symbols and beliefs continued to exist, but they were perhaps recorded on perishable items and consequently were not preserved for archaeological interpretation. Some of these symbols, slightly altered, appear during the post–A.D. 1000 Mississippian florescence. The post-Hopewellian regionalization may be related to the growth of complex sedentary societies.

As during earlier times some of the best evidence from this period for the use of black drink or other medicines comes from Florida. In the burial mounds of the St. Johns River culture of eastern Florida, dated at A.D. 800 to A.D. 1000, shell cups are quite common.[30] There is evidence for continual contact between this area and the cultures of northwest and north Florida at this time, and shell cups and other religious paraphernalia may have been traded back and forth. At the Tick Island mound in Volusia County, C. B. Moore recovered two clay vessels, one of which was shaped like a shell cup and the other like a *Busycon* shell with the spikes intact.[31] One burial in the mound was accompanied by a shell cup that was covered with a large potsherd, possibly to protect the contents from dirt when the burial was covered with earth.

In Alachua County, Florida, William H. Sears's excavations at the Melton Mound no. 3, a north-central Florida Weeden Island–affiliated mound dating from ca. A.D. 500 to A.D. 600, revealed a large "pathway" or linear deposit of large broken ceramic vessels and one broken shell cup. The presence of secondary burials in the mound indicates that the bodies were cleaned and then stored elsewhere, probably in a charnel house, and then placed in the mound in a single ceremony along with the pottery and shell cup deposit. Possibly this is an example of the ritual cleaning-out of charnel house sacred objects described above.[32]

At the McKenzie mound on Lake Weir in Marion County, in central Florida, Sears found secondary burials placed together in the mound during a single interment and construction ceremony.[33] Again, use of a charnel house is indicated. An offering of a single skull burial, one double skull burial (perhaps trophy skulls from warfare), an infant sacrificial burial, and a shell cup, were placed in the mound on its east side. A separate cache containing a number of miniature ceramic vessels, a bottle-shaped vessel, one deep pot, several bowls, and a shell cup was also present in the mound. Sears notes that this particular set of vessels and containers strongly suggests that they were used for the brewing of black drink.[34] Among the historic southeastern tribes several types of ceremonial teas or medicines were brewed in addition to black drink. The water bottles and the gourd-shaped vessels from this and other sites may have served as containers for these other drinks.

In northwest Florida following the Green Point complex, after about A.D. 500, shell cups continued to be placed with mortuary vessels in burial mounds, both as grave goods and in separate caches. The distribution of shell cups during this time ranges from the Alabama border southward to Charlotte Harbor on the lower Florida coast. C. B. Moore, Gordon R. Willey, and others, have here excavated a large number of Weeden Island burial mounds containing shell cups.[35]

Possible evidence for black drink or similar ceremonies also comes from two Weeden Island mounds. The first is the Davis Field mound in Calhoun County, a mound constructed with a secondary mound placed on top of the primary mound. On the surface of the first mound a small circular rise of earth 1.5 feet high and 7 feet in diameter was constructed before the second mound was added. Three bowls were placed on the top of this small mound. A hearth was placed immediately adjacent to the small mound, also on the primary mound surface, and two shell cups were found lying on the side of the small mound. Together these objects and their position on top of the primary mound suggest that a drink ritual was performed before the secondary mound cap was added.[36]

A special group of pottery vessels and shell cups was found associated with a fire hearth on a primary mound surface at the Hope mound north of Tampa Bay, as they had been at the Davis Field site.[37] The vessels included a pan-shaped vessel (possibly for parching leaves), a miniature pot with a killed bottom, three gourd-shaped water jars (one killed), a killed bowl, a large bowl, and six shell cups. One of the shell cups lay over a trophy skull, and one was covered with a large flat stone, perhaps to protect its contents. In addition, a large deep vessel was found in situ on a hearth. These vessels and the hearth were covered with a secondary mound quite similar to the one at the Davis Field site, again suggesting a ceremony involving brewing and drinking of sacred medicines. The ceremonies represented by these two Weeden Island culture examples are reminiscent of the burial scene portrayed by Le Moyne in which shell cups were placed on the surface of the burial mound containing the remains of Timucua Indians (fig. 5).[38]

Although the possible use of black drink and the use of ceremonial shell drinking cups are best documented for post-Hopewellian times in Florida, this may be due to the quantity of archaeological research carried out rather than the cultural distribution of the trait per se. However, ceremonial use of a drink appears to have a wide distribution in Florida where *Ilex vomitoria* is common, reflecting, perhaps, the taking of black drink on frequent occasions. Research into other southeastern cultures of this time period is needed to verify and describe the possible use of black drink elsewhere.

MISSISSIPPIAN AND PROTO-HISTORIC PERIOD— POST–A.D. 1000

By A.D. 1000 a new way of life had developed among many of the peoples in the eastern United States. This Mississippian cultural tradition was characterized by complex sociopolitical organization and intensive maize and bean horticulture. Beans, probably a late introduction from Mesoamerica, provided a domesticated source of plant protein.

The religion of these Mississippian peoples appears to have been intimately connected with their social organization and with their interest in horticultural fertility. Societies were stratified into ranked classes, with groups of nobles headed by priest-chiefs who resided at large ceremonial centers which were in part economically supported by outlying horticultural villages. Such centers, characterized by elaborate mounds, villages, and earthworks, are well known in the East, especially in the piedmont and plateau region of the Southeast and the Mississippi River Valley. Individual political units (chiefdoms) were bound together by religious and political beliefs and practices.

By about A.D. 1200 the Southeast had become surprisingly homogeneous with respect to symbols, art motifs, objects, and practices associated with religion and sociopolitical organization. This complex of traits, known as the Southern Cult, was originally thought by some archaeologists to have been associated with a nativistic movement that swept through the Southeast as a result of the intrusion of early European contact, perhaps the Hernando de Soto *entrada*. Their argument was that the Southern Cult was similar to the Ghost Dance which swept much of the western United States in the nineteenth century. Now, however, it is generally accepted that the Southern Cult represents the material expression of beliefs concerning social and political practices, including warfare, social stratification, and the relationships that existed between people and their gods.

This Mississippian cult, as evidenced by the spread of very similar (at times identical) symbols and other paraphernalia into many parts of the Southeast, may have been directly diffused by prophets, missionaries, or other specialized religious functionaries, or through other forms of direct contact, such as warfare. Objects, probably manufactured at a few centers, were widely traded.

Unfortunately, archaeology is incapable of telling us about the specific behavior associated with the black drink ritual in the Southern Cult–Mississippian "religion," although we can suggest contexts in which it was used, such as in purification ceremonies of the Creek and other historic southeastern tribes. Use in burial rituals probably also continued. It is possible that when the practice of mound burial was discontinued by many southeastern tribes, sometime shortly before or after contact with Europeans, black drink was no longer used in burial ceremonies, if indeed it ever had been.

As mentioned previously, both plain and highly decorated shell cups are characteristic of the Southern Cult, and usually the decorated cups are engraved with cult symbols. When the numbers of such cups found at Mississippian sites are compared with those found at Formative sites, it is obvious that along with the Mississippian cultural florescence there was an increase in the uses of the cups, or black drink, or both. Perhaps this is a reflection of the adoption of black drink into nonburial purification rituals, or perhaps it may even reflect the first use of the drink. It is also during this period that cups are found for the first time with structures not associated with burials.

Distribution of Mississippian shell cups is so widespread that only a few notable examples illustrating geographical distribution and forms of occurrence will be discussed here.[39] C. B. Moore's early excavations at the Moundville mound complex site in central Alabama revealed evidence of a black drink ritual similar to those described above for the Weeden Island culture in Florida.[40] In one mound he unearthed a shell cup with a ceramic vessel inverted over it to serve as a cover. In the shell cup was a black organic residue that was present also in clay pots from the site. This substance may have been similar to the black fluid rings found in a shell cup from Oklahoma, which are thought to have resulted from the evaporation of black drink from the cup.

Near the Moundville shell cup and inverted vessel were a water bottle and a crudely made cooking vessel with two loop handles. This paraphernalia probably was used to brew, pour, and drink black drink in a burial ritual. At the same site another burial was accompanied by a water bottle, a bowl, a broad-mouthed water bottle, and a shell cup, again suggesting the use of black drink.[41] Other shell cups, some engraved, came from various mounds and burials on the site.[42] More recent excavations at the site have revealed numerous other burials with ceramic water bottles and shell cups. At least one ceramic conch-shell effigy vessel has been found; and miniature or toy vessels, perhaps for other medicines, frequently were found with shell cups.[43]

Shell cups, some of which are engraved with cult symbols, have been recovered from the Etowah mound complex site in northwestern Georgia[44] and from the Macon ceremonial center in central Georgia.[45] At both sites the cups were in burial mounds. Cups have also been found at the Kolomoki mound complex in southwestern Georgia. The Kolomoki people seem to have practiced a burial ceremony quite similar to that recorded for the historic Natchez Indians of Louisiana.[46] All three of these sites were probably occupied by ancestors of various Muskogean-speaking tribes.

At the Irene site near Savannah, Georgia, cups were found associated with burials in several mounds at the site.[47] Often the cups were perforated in the "beak." In one of the Irene mounds, archaeologists uncovered evidence of a large circular rotunda, some 120 feet in diameter, within a walled enclosure. Outside of the structure, but within the enclosure, was a pottery dump where vessels were broken and discarded. The authors suggest that a black drink ceremony was held in the rotunda, which was evidently constructed like those structures described for the historic Creek and Cherokee Indians, and that the ceramic drinking or brewing vessels used in the ritual were smashed afterward and discarded in a sacred place. This is quite similar to what is thought to have happened among some of the prehistoric Florida cultures.

Among the Mississippian cultures of Tennessee shell cups were also common. According to Lewis and Kneberg, "Practically all sites with Dallas components [a late Mississippian culture thought to be associated with the protohistoric Cherokee] have produced one or more of these vessels [shell cups] which are usually associated with burials."[48] At Hiwassee Island, a site on the Tennessee River, a shell cup was excavated on the floor of Building 25, a rectangular structure containing a doorway entrance paved with flagstones, a clay seat, two rectangular fireplaces, and three floor storage pits (for sacred medicines?).[49] Probably this was a ceremonial meeting structure similar to the Irene rotunda where black drink was ritually consumed.

At the Mount Royal Mississippian mound site in the Florida St. Johns area, C. B. Moore excavated 1,307 *Busycon* shells.[50] Only a few of the shells had been made into cups, but the large number suggests that the shells had special significance. The shells were placed in mound caches, with 136 of them in the largest cache. One pottery cache in the mound contained two vessels with handles like those shown in the Le Moyne drawings picturing the St. Johns region Timucua Indians preparing black drink.[51] These two vessels were accompanied by four other vessels, all placed close together and covered with a large dish-shaped ceramic vessel. Again, these possibly represent the paraphernalia for a black drink ritual or for brewing other sacred medicines common to the Southeast. The number of vessels (four) could correspond to the four sacred teas present among many of the southeastern tribes.[52]

C. B. Moore and Gordon Willey both report Safety Harbor culture sites in the Tampa Bay region with shell cups accompanying burials.[53] In several instances these cups were found along with European artifacts, indicating a historic period provenience for some of the cups. The late Safety Harbor archaeological culture was associated with the historic Tocobaga Indians encountered in the sixteenth century by the Hernando de Soto and Pánfilo de Narváez expeditions. Moore also reports shell cups from a historic Charlotte Harbor site which must have been inhabited by the Calusa Indians.[54] Frank Cush-

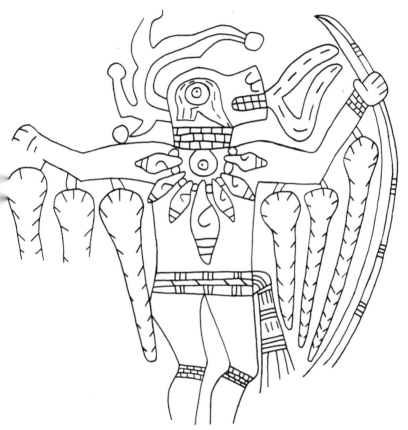

Figure 9. Eagle Man motif from figure 8. Note the perforated shells suspended from the necklace. Courtesy of the Smithsonian Institution National Museum of Natural History.

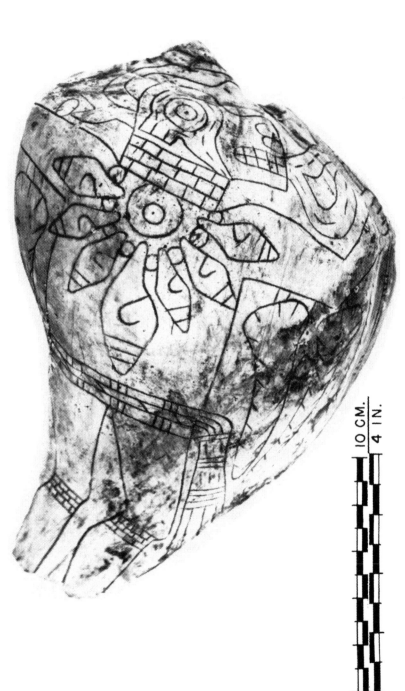

Figure 8. Shell cup engraved with Eagle Man motif. Courtesy of the Smithsonian Institution, National Museum of Natural History, Department of Anthropology.

10 CM.

4 IN.

ing's investigations at the Key Marco site, also in southwestern Florida, revealed fifty-five *Busycon* cups. Most likely, Key Marco was associated with protohistoric or historic Calusa.[55]

Perhaps the most famous shell cups are those found at the Mississippian-period Craig mound at the Spiro site in eastern Oklahoma. Actually composed of four connected mounds, the Craig mound was systematically looted by the Picola Mining Company, a group of six collectors who sold the artifacts that they had dug from the mound. A vast collection of shell, stone, bone, metal, pottery, feather, and textile goods was taken from a central cache in the mound (probably a burial charnel house floor) where the natural settling of the soft objects, such as blankets, created a large cavern in the sand and clay matrix of the mound's center. This air-free "cavern" preserved what ordinarily would have been perishable objects. The story of these first "excavations" at the mound and the artifacts collected has been related by Forest E. Clements and Henry W. Hamilton.[56]

Later excavations at the site (1936–1941) were carried out by the University of Oklahoma and the Works Projects Administration. Recently, James A. Brown has collated much of the Spiro data.[57] However, little information survives concerning the associations of the shell cups with other artifacts in the cache. Brown has noted a correlation between shell cups, shell ornaments, copper sheets, and litter burials.[58] Most likely the persons buried on litters represented the priest-chiefs of the noble class and the members of their families. Conch shell cups, but not the other symbols of rank and status, were also frequently found with persons of lower status.

Estimates of the number of shell cups taken from the mound by the Picola Mining Company range from sixty-five to one hundred. Most of the cups were engraved. A sample of fourteen of these cups stored at the Heye Foundation in New York, range in length from $8\frac{3}{8}$ inches to $13\frac{1}{2}$ inches with a mean of $11\frac{5}{8}$ inches.[59] Pictures of the engravings found on these and other shell cups have been widely published,[60] and their significance to the symbolism of the Southern Cult usages of black drink has been studied.[61] One cup (specimen 18/9082 at the Heye Foundation) has a series of fluid rings, each successively darker toward the bottom of the cup. These rings probably are the result of slow evaporation of the liquid contents, causing increased sedimentation of the remaining liquid. Anyone who has left a partially filled coffee cup in the office over a long weekend has witnessed a similar process. This ringed specimen is from the central chamber of the Craig mound, suggesting that black drink offerings in shell drinking cups were placed with burials in mounds, a practice possibly dating back nearly two thousand years to the early Formative period. Interestingly, one of the ceramic vessels from the Craig mound is shaped like a shell cup, also an old southeastern trait.[62]

At least eight of the engravings on the Spiro cups show a ceremony thought to be either the Muskogean busk dance, celebrating the summer harvest, or the southeastern stick-ball game. Frequently this cult motif is labeled "Choosing Up Sides," because the figures seem to be choosing sides for the stick-ball game by grasping a baseball bat (see fig. 10c). Alice L. Mariott of the Indian Arts and Crafts Board, Oklahoma City, offers the following interpretation of this particular motif:

It seems possible that the ceremony represented might have some connection with the 'busk' or harvest festival that was so widely distributed through the Southeastern tribes. An essential part of the busk is a group of men's dances around a central pole. In some tribes the pole is topped with a representational carving of a fish, bird, or animal, while in others it is simply a post set in the ground. Another feature of the busk is a men's ballgame, played with racquet-like cleft sticks. For this game, the men strip down to breech-clouts and belts, and play barefoot. The belt and breech-clout belonging to a player are very important, and are kept with his stick, all tied together and most carefully put away between games.

One feature of all Southeastern ceremonials seems to have been the "black drink," a fairly violent emetic which was taken before,

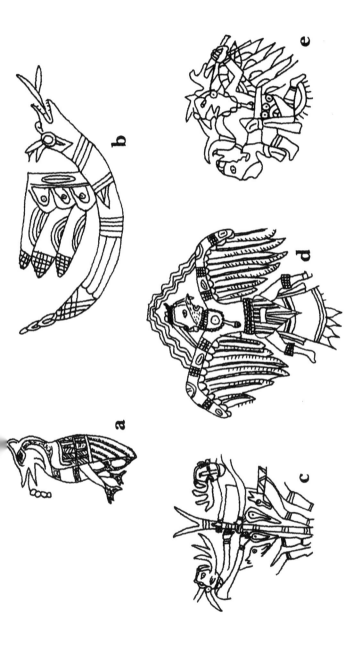

Figure 10. Southern Cult motifs. **a.** Woodpecker with "speech" scroll. **b.** Bird-serpent with scroll. **c.** "Choosing Up Sides" motif. **d, e.** Eagle Man motifs with perforated shell cups suspended from necklaces. (All from Waring and Holder, "Ceremonial Complex.")

during, and after the performance of the ritual. It is remotely possible that the "balloons" issuing from the mouths of the figures represent the effect of this dose. They could just as well represent human speech.[63]

Other "speech scrolls"—either bi- or tri-forked scrolls or groups of three or four balls—are present in the cult motifs, especially with the god-animal representations such as the woodpecker, bird-serpent, and masked dancers.[64] The scrolls, which do not appear with the eagle-being motif, might, as Mariott suggests, represent vomiting as a result of a black drink purification ceremony (see fig. 10 a,b,c).

The eagle-being figure, evidently not pictured in cult symbolism as a receiver of black drink, might represent the giver or passer of the drink, whose role is portrayed during black drink ceremonials by a special individual. Examination of the eagle-being motif shows that the figure wears a shell necklace from which a shell cup is suspended (see fig. 10 d,e; figs. 8–9). Suspension of the cup from the neck would explain the perforations found in the small ends of many of the vessels, as described above. Possibly the eagle-being was viewed as the giver of life or fertility (in this case black drink), who passed it on to animals, man, and the natural elements, all represented by the various motifs with scrolls. This ritual, the passing of black drink in shell cups suspended from the neck, was reenacted in the ceremonies of the southeastern tribes.

SUMMARY

The earliest use of shell cups was among the Archaic cultures of the Tennessee and Ohio river drainages at about 5000 B.C. For the Archaic people, marine shell was an exotic item and was traded to these areas from the southern coasts. During the period of the Hopewellian complex, shell cups were also traded inland, and they apparently took on significance beyond being simply valued items. A possible association between *Ilex vomitoria* leaves and shell cups may have resulted from their being

traded together. Drink paraphernalia might have been ex-
changed in the North for the exotic animal teeth, mortuary
pottery, copper and stone ornaments, and other artifacts that
archaeologists have found at southern sites.

Although Hopewellian use of black drink is speculative, it
was common practice for a few special individuals, perhaps
priests, chiefs, or head-traders, to have cups interred with them
in burial mounds, indicating, perhaps, the presence of a drinking ritual. Association of the cups with mortuary pottery in
Florida suggests that utensils used in the preparation of such
a drink were broken and discarded after use and that periodically these were placed in caches in burial mounds. There is
evidence that during and after the Hopewellian period a drinking ceremony was performed at an early stage in mound construction and upon the occasion of depositing pottery caches
in mounds. Probably such a ceremony was involved with the
burying of burials previously cleaned and stored in a charnel
house. The presence of several types of bottle- and gourd-
shaped vessels and other brewing paraphernalia with shell cups
could reflect the use of more than one ceremonial tea.

During the Mississippian period we have strong evidence for
the use of black drink with shell cups in burial ceremonials
and, for the first time, in purification rituals such as the stick-
ball game and busk ceremony. The development of the Southern Cult and its beliefs and rituals was probably not a rapid
process but the gradual reformulation and elaboration of
indigenous beliefs and practices in the presence of a new extensive horticultural economy and more complex forms of
social organization. A traditional drinking ritual, perhaps dating back to Hopewellian times, probably became a part of cult
ceremonialism. But whether black drink was a part of this
traditional practice or a Mississippian addition is not certain.
Many of the Mississippian beliefs and practices, including
black drink, were still present in the Southeast when the first
Europeans arrived, and in some regions these elements of
southeastern Indian culture survived into the nineteenth century.

NOTES

1. For a summary of the relationships (or lack of them) between Mesoamerica and the eastern United States, see James B. Griffin, "Mesoamerica and the Eastern United States in Prehistoric Times," in *Archaeological Frontiers and External Connections*, eds. G. Ekholm and G. R. Willey, Handbook of Middle American Indians, vol. 4 (Austin: University of Texas Press, 1966), pp. 111–31.

2. Information on shell species and distributions is based on R. Tucker Abbott, *American Seashells* (New York: Van Nostrand, 1974), and H. Stephen Hale, "Marine Shells in Midwestern Archaeological Sites and the Determination of their Most Probable Source" (Master's thesis, Florida Atlantic University, 1976).

3. See William H. Sears, "The Hopewellian Affiliations of Certain Sites on the Gulf Coast of Florida," *American Antiquity* 28 (1962): 5–18; James H. Kellar, A. R. Kelly, and E. V. McMichael, "The Mandeville Site in Southwest Georgia," *American Antiquity* 28 (1962): 338–55; Clarence B. Moore, "Certain Aboriginal Mounds of the Florida Central-West Coast," *Journal of the Academy of Natural Sciences* 12 (1903): 363–431; idem, "Mounds of the Lower Chattahoochee and Lower Flint Rivers," *Journal of the Academy of Natural Sciences* 13 (1907): 426–57; idem, "The Northwestern Florida Coast Revisited," *Journal of the Academy of Natural Sciences* 16 (1918): 514–74.

4. William S. Webb, *The Carlson Annis Mound, Site 5, Butler County, Kentucky*, University of Kentucky Reports in Anthropology, vol. 7, no. 4 (Lexington, 1950).

5. W. S. Webb, *Indian Knoll, Site Oh-2, Ohio County, Kentucky*, University of Kentucky Reports in Anthropology and Archaeology, vol. 4, no. 3, pt. 1 (Lexington, 1946).

6. William H. Claflin, Jr., *The Stalling's Island Mound, Columbia County, Georgia*, Papers of the Peabody Museum of American Archaeology and Ethnology, Harvard University, vol. 14, no. 1 (Cambridge, 1931), p. 27.

7. James A. Ford and Clarence H. Webb, *Poverty Point: A Late Archaic Site in Louisiana*, Anthropological Papers of the American Museum of Natural History, vol. 46, pt. 1 (New York, 1956).

8. J. A. Ford and George I. Quimby, *The Tchefuncte Culture, an Early Occupation of the Lower Mississippi Valley*, Society for American Archaeology Memoir no. 2 (Menasha, 1945), pp. 50–51.

9. For a brief description of early horticulture in the Okeechobee Basin see W. H. Sears, "Food Production and Village Life in Prehistoric Southeastern United States," *Archaeology* 24 (1971): 322–29.

10. The Hopewell or mound-builder culture of the Midwest is different from the Hopewellian complex found through the East after A.D. 1. The Hopewellian complex was first described on the basis of the midwestern Hopewell culture, which provided the source for its name. But the complex, with its associated behavior patterns, might not have originated among the northern Hopewell peoples. Current research in Florida is yielding more and more evidence of the early development of complex social organization associated with widespread trade and maize horticulture in the Okeechobee Basin and a later spread into northwestern and northern regions of the state. Previous research has also shown early development of complex ceremonialism at the Poverty Point site in Louisiana. The Hopewellian complex may have resulted from a blending of regional cultural traditions brought together by the trade of exotic high-status items. Knowledge of maize horticultural methods and the seeds themselves may have been traded within the Hopewellian interaction sphere.

11. James B. Griffin, "Culture Periods in Eastern United States Archeology," in *Archeology of Eastern United States,* ed. J. B. Griffin (Chicago: University of Chicago Press, 1952), p. 360.

12. See Olaf H. Prufer, *The McGraw Site: A Study in Hopewellian Dynamics,* Cleveland Museum of Natural History Scientific Papers, n.s., vol. 5 (Cleveland, 1965).

13. Examples of this practice can be found at mound 11 of the Havanna group and also at the Kemp site, both in the Illinois River Valley. See Frank C. Baker et al., *Contributions to the Archeology of the Illinois River Valley,* Transactions of the American Philosophical Society, vol. 32, pt. 1 (Philadelphia, 1941).

14. Georg K. Neumann and Melvin L. Fowler, "Hopewellian Sites in the Lower Wabash Valley," in *Hopewellian Communities in Illinois,* ed. T. Deuel, Illinois State Museum Scientific Papers, vol. 5 (Springfield, 1952), pp. 175–248.

15. Richard G. Morgan, "Outline of Cultures in the Ohio Region," in *Archeology of Eastern United States,* ed. J. B. Griffin (Chicago: University of Chicago Press, 1952), pp. 83–98. J. A. Ford and Gordon Willey, *Crooks Site: A Marksville Period Burial Mound in LaSalle Parish, Louisiana,* Department of Conservation, Louisiana Geological Society Anthropological Study no. 3 (New Orleans, 1940).

16. James A. Ford, *Hopewell Culture Burial Mounds near Helena, Arkansas,* Anthropological Papers of the American Museum of Natural History, vol. 50, pt. 1 (New York, 1963).

17. For example, at the Ross Site, as reported by W. S. Webb and Charles G. Wilder, *An Archeological Survey of Guntersville Basin on the Tennessee River in Northern Alabama* (Lexington: University of Kentucky Press, 1951), pl. 35.

18. Sears, "Hopewellian Affiliations," pp. 5–18.

19. C. B. Moore, "Certain Aboriginal Remains of the Northwest Florida Coast," *Journal of the Academy of Natural Sciences* 13 (1907): 406–25.

20. C. B. Moore, "Certain Aboriginal Mounds of the Apalachicola River," *Journal of the Academy of Natural Sciences* 12 (1903): 473–74.

21. Moore, "Northwest Florida Coast," pp. 265–74; idem, "Crystal River Revisited," *Journal of the Academy of Natural Sciences* 13 (1907): 406–25.

22. Vessel 37 in Moore, "Northwest Florida Coast," fig. 226.

23. Ibid., pp. 217–29.

24. For example, see specimens from Fannings Bayou, in Moore, "Northwest Florida Coast," pp. 152–59.

25. Moore, "Northwest Florida Coast"; Moore, "Florida Central-West Coast"; Moore, "Apalachicola River"; Moore, "Moundville"; Moore, "Northwestern Florida Coast Revisited."

26. "Mesoamerican Glyph Motifs on Southeastern Pottery," in *Verhandlungen des XXXVIII. Internationalen Amerikanistenkongress, Band 11, Stuttgart-München, 12. bis 18. August 1968* (Munich: Kommissionsverlag Klaus Renner, 1970), pp. 89–99.

27. For discussion of similarities between southeastern and Mesoamerican ceramics see E. V. McMichael, "Veracruz, the Crystal River Complex, and the Hopewellian Climax," in *Hopewell Studies*, eds. J. R. Caldwell and R. L. Hall, Illinois State Museum Scientific Papers, vol. 12 (Springfield, 1964), pp. 123–32; Griffin, "Mesoamerica and the Eastern United States in Prehistoric Times," pp. 111–31.

28. Phelps, "Glyph Motifs," pp. 98–99.

29. J. E. S. Thompson, *Maya Hieroglyphic Writing*, 2d ed., (Norman: University of Oklahoma Press, 1960).

30. C. B. Moore, "Certain Sand Mounds of the St. Johns River, Florida," *Journal of the Academy of Natural Sciences*, vol. 10, pts. 1 and 2 (1894).

31. Ibid., pl. 15, item 1; fig. 42, p. 69.

32. William H. Sears, "Melton Mound Number 3," *Florida Anthropologist* 9 (1956): 87–100.

33. William H. Sears, *Two Weeden Island Period Burial Mounds*, Contributions of the Florida State Museum, Social Sciences, no. 5 (Gainesville, 1959).

34. Ibid., p. 34.

35. Moore, "Northwestern Florida Coast"; Moore, "Florida Central-West Coast"; Moore, "Apalachicola River"; Moore, "Northwestern Florida Coast Revisited"; G. R. Willey, *Archeology of the*

Florida Gulf Coast, Smithsonian Miscellaneous Collections, vol. 113 (Washington, D.C., 1949).

36. Moore, "Apalachicola River," pp. 468–73.

37. Samuel D. Smith, "Excavations at the Hope Mound with an Addendum to the Stafford Mound Report," *Florida Anthropologist* 14 (1971): 107–34.

38. Stefan Lorant, *The New World* (New York: Duel, Sloane, and Pearce, 1946).

39. The extent of this contact is indicated by the presence of marine shells as far north as the Mississippian site of Aztalan, east of Madison, Wisconsin. See S. A. Barrett, *Ancient Aztalan,* Public Museum of the City of Milwaukee Bulletin no. 13 (Milwaukee, 1933). Shell cups have been found as far north as the Cahokia site in southwestern Illinois. See Warren K. Moorehead, *The Cahokia Mounds,* University of Illinois Bulletin, vol. 26, no. 4 (Urbana, 1928).

40. C. B. Moore, "Certain Aboriginal Remains of the Black Warrior River," *Journal of the Academy of Natural Sciences* 13 (1905): 125–244.

41. Ibid., p. 223.

42. C. B. Moore, "Moundville Revisited," *Journal of the Academy of Natural Sciences* 13 (1907): 336–405.

43. An excellent analysis and interpretation of the Moundsville site social organization, including descriptions of burial goods, can be found in Christopher S. Peebles, 'Moundville, the organization of a Prehistoric Community and Culture," (Ph.D. diss., University of California at Santa Barbara, 1974).

44. W. K. Moorehead, "Exploration of the Etowah Site in Georgia," in *Etowah Papers,* ed. W. K. Moorehead (New Haven: Yale University Press, 1932), pp. 76, 80, 94; Lewis H. Larson, Jr., "Archaeological Implications of Social Stratification at the Etowah Site, Georgia," in *Approaches to the Social Dimensions of Mortuary Practices,* ed. James A. Brown, Society for American Archaeology Memoir no. 25 (Menasha, 1971), pp. 58–67.

45. Charles H. Fairbanks, "Creek and Pre-Creek," in *Archeology of Eastern United States,* ed. J. B. Griffin (Chicago: University of Chicago Press, 1952), pp. 290–93.

46. W. H. Sears, "An Archeological Manifestation of a Natchez-type Burial Ceremony," *Florida Anthropologist* 5 (1952): 1–7; idem, *Excavations at Kolomoki—A Final Report,* University of Georgia Series in Anthropology, no. 5 (Athens, 1956).

47. Joseph R. Caldwell and Catherine McCann, *Irene Mound Site, Chatham County, Georgia* (Athens: University of Georgia Press, 1941), pl. 19, k.

48. T. M. N. Lewis and Madeline Kneberg, *Hiwassee Island,* 2d ed. (Knoxville: University of Tennessee Press, 1970), p. 131.

49. Ibid., pl. 23, fig. 3.

50. Moore, "St. Johns River," p. 29.

51. Ibid., pl. 5, items 3–4.

52. John R. Swanton, *Religious Beliefs and Medicinal Practices of the Creek Indians,* Smithsonian Institution Forty-second Annual Report (Washington, D.C., 1928), pp. 546–614.

53. Moore, "Florida Central-West Coast," pp. 434–36; Willey, *Florida Gulf Coast,* pp. 152–56, 337.

54. C. B. Moore, "Miscellaneous Investigations in Florida," *Journal of the Academy of Natural Sciences* 13 (1905): 302.

55. Marion S. Gilliland, *The Material Culture of Key Marco, Florida* (Gainesville: University Presses of Florida, 1975).

56. Forest E. Clements, "Historical Sketch of the Spiro Mound," Museum of the American Indian, Heye Foundation Contributions, no. 14 (New York, 1945), pp. 48–68; Henry W. Hamilton, "The Spiro Mound," *Missouri Archaeologist* 14 (1952): 17–88.

57. James A. Brown and Robert E. Bell, *Report on the First Year's Analysis of the Spiro Mound Group, LeFlore County, Oklahoma,* First Annual Report of Caddoan Archeology—Spiro Focus Research (Norman: University of Oklahoma Research Institute, 1964); J. A. Brown, *Spiro Studies, Volume I, Description of the Mound Group,* First Part of the Second Annual Report of Caddoan Archeology—Spiro Focus Research (Norman: University of Oklahoma Research Institute, 1966); idem, *Spiro Studies, Volume II, the Graves and Their Contents,* Second Part of the Second Annual Report of Caddoan Archeology —Spiro Focus Research (Norman: University of Oklahoma Research Institute, 1966); idem, "The Dimensions of Status in the Burials at Spiro," in *Approaches to the Social Dimensions of Mortuary Practices,* ed. J. A. Brown, pp. 58–67.

58. Brown, "Burials at Spiro," p. 101.

59. These measurements are taken from E. K. Burnett, "The Spiro Mound Collection in the Museum," Museum of the American Indian, Heye Foundation Contributions, no. 14 (New York, 1945), pls. 27–57.

60. For pictures of the cups, see Burnett, "Spiro Collection"; Hamilton, "Spiro Mound"; or Emma Lila Fundaburk and Mary D. F. Foreman, eds., *Sun Circles and Human Hands* (Luverne, Ala.: E. L. Fundaburk, 1957).

61. Discussions of Southern Cult symbols can be found in A. J. Waring, Jr., and Preston Holder, "A Prehistoric Ceremonial Complex in the Southeastern United States," *American Anthropologist* 47 (1945): 1–34; and in A. J. Waring Jr., "The Southern Cult and Mus-

khogean Ceremonial," in *The Waring Papers,* ed. S. Williams (Athens: University of Georgia Press, 1968), pp. 30–69.

62. Hamilton, "Spiro Mound," pl. 32a.
63. Quote taken from Hamilton, "Spiro Mound," p. 64.
64. See Waring and Holder, "Prehistoric Ceremonial Complex."

The Function of Black Drink
among the Creeks

Charles H. Fairbanks

While all, or most, southeastern Indians used black drink in ceremonial situations, it was especially important among the numerous tribes or "towns" that made up the Creek Confederacy in colonial times. Thus it is pertinent to examine the role that this ritual tea played in the daily and ceremonial lives of the Creeks. Clearly it must have had a long history among these Indians because it was thoroughly integrated into their daily lives and into the deliberations of their town elders and chiefs. When one examines this trait through time, however, only tantalizing hints can be found.

The Creeks were a major element in the southeastern Indian population, inhabiting a large area within what is now the states of Georgia and Alabama. At the dawn of the colonial period their ancestors were quite thickly settled along the coasts of Georgia, very numerous in the interior parts of Georgia and Alabama, and less thickly settled in the Carolina piedmont. While they used the fire climax pine forest of the coastal plain for hunting, they seem to have had few if any towns there. Most of the larger towns were located along the edge of the piedmont, where the fall line intersects the Savannah, Oconee, Ocmulgee, Flint, Chattahoochee, Coosa, and Tallapoosa rivers. With a subsistence pattern based on corn, beans, and pumpkin agriculture, these towns were elaborate permanent villages, often housing several hundred people. Smaller satellite hamlets were frequently scattered between the larger towns. Almost always the towns were located near the fall line, adjacent to fertile silt loams in the vicinity of an ecotone where several biomes could be exploited.[1]

As yet there has been a scarcity of historical archeology directly aimed at tracing the antecedents of Creek culture into the prehistoric period. It is clear, however, that the Mississippian phase in the south must be directly or indirectly ancestral to the culture of the Creeks.[2] The Mississippian phase occupied the same geographic range as did the Creeks, often the same specific sites. The Mississippian phase saw the introduction of full-blown agriculture, and it contains a number of specific cultural traits that persist into the historic era. The earliest representative of the Mississippian pattern in central Georgia is the Macon Plateau phase, well represented by the type site and the nearby Brown's Mount site. There are indications that the Macon Plateau site contains items which strongly imply the use of black drink. At Mound C on the western edge of the large fortified village, conch cups found among the burials are believed to be evidence of the use of black drink. One of the large complex burials precedent to the construction of the first mound stage contained the remains of at least seven individuals. Among the numerous grave goods, a conch shell cup rested on top of the mass of bones. Another conch shell cup was found with the bones of an adult buried in the slope of the fourth mound stage. Two large unmodified conch shells were found with other burials. In addition there were a number of hooded ceramic bottles with burials. While we cannot directly relate these to black drink ritual, they certainly do suggest the importance of liquids as burial accompaniments.[3]

A prominent feature of the Macon Plateau phase was the presence of numerous circular earthlodges which clearly had a ritual use. In the largest of these, a large pottery bowl was found on the floor under the burned debris of the superstructure. Again, we cannot with certainty relate this to the use of black drink, but it does strongly suggest the ritual use of a drink in the building. A number of the earthlodges at Macon Plateau, and one earthlodge at Brown's Mount, had raised clay benches along the circular outside walls. In front of each seat was an oval clay depression which may possibly have been used

as a vomitive basin. There is no clear evidence as to the use of
these basins, but again, there seems to be a suggestion that they
were used in connection with black drink.[4]

While the Macon Plateau phase represents a relatively pure
expression of Mississippian elements, subsequent phases show
considerable admixture of Late Mississippian and local Southern Appalachian Stamped Tradition traits. These phases,
Lamar, Willbanks, Irene, and so on, generally include strong
Southern Cult elements, and conch shell cups are common.
The Lamar phase, at least, must on the basis of distribution
and relationship to later phases, represent the material culture
of Creek or Muskogean groups in the immediately prehistoric
periods of the fifteenth and sixteenth centuries. No very detailed excavations of Lamar phase sites have been published.
But for our purposes here it is sufficient to call attention to
conch shell cups at several Lamar sites, as well as the regular
presence of ceramic bottle forms, some of them having the
forms of elaborate effigies. There seems to have been no other
use for these bottle forms than to contain liquids, and they are
rather frequently found in burials. The Lamar phase is also
notable for the great increase in the number of clay tobacco
pipes and pipe fragments. From their distribution in household
and midden situations there is a strong suggestion that smoking had become habitual, a change from the solely ritual pattern of earlier times. In view of the fact that black drink and
tobacco were intimately associated among the Creeks, this may
be a significant observation.

Among the historic Creeks black drink was regularly used
both in major ceremonials and in daily social contexts. It is
often listed first among the four especially sacred teas or medicines of the Creeks. As the social use of black drink was more
often observed by Europeans than the use of other teas, accounts of the use of black drink are by far the most common.
In its ceremonial use, it was one of the four great medicines
used in the annual busk or green corn ceremonial held in early
summer. The following were the major medicinal teas.

1. *Assi,* or black drink, prepared from the leaves of yaupon holly (*Ilex vomitoria* Ait.).

2. *Miko hoyanidja,* or "passer by of the chiefs," made from the pounded roots of a species of willow (probably *Salix nigra* March., *S. Carolina* Michx., or hybrids of these). *Miko hoyanidja* seems to have been regarded as the most potent of the four medicines, perhaps because it contained salicylic acid, related to modern aspirin.

3. *Pasa,* made from the pounded roots of button snakeroot (*Eryngium yuccifolium* Michx.), often called the "war physic" by Europeans. This may have been poisonous in large doses. It is described, however, as producing a sense of peace and tranquility.

4. *Hilis hatki,* which the Creeks called "white medicine," but known to us as ginseng (*Panax quinquefolium* L.). Again, the pounded roots were used to brew a tea.

Aside from the common southeastern Indian preference for groups of four, it is perhaps notable that *assi* or black drink differs from the other busk medicines in several ways. It is the only one prepared from the leaves of the plant; the others are brewed from pounded roots. It is also apparently the only one which was heated or toasted before being steeped. Even though it was the only one not naturally occurring along the fall-line habitat of most Creek towns, it was the only tea which was widely used as a daily drink, as will be discussed later.

Used in a number of ritual situations, among the Creeks black drink seems always to have served as a preparatory purifying drink in advance of special ritual situations. This common theme is reflected by Caleb Swan when he says:

Except rum there is no liquor of which the Creek Indians are so excessively fond. In addition to their habitual fondness for it, they have a religious belief that it infallibly possesses the following qualities, viz.: That it purifies them from all sin, and leaves them in a state of perfect innocence; that it inspires them with an invincible prowess in war; and that it is the only solid cement of friendship, benevolence, and hospitality.[5]

According to Benjamin Hawkins, black drink was consumed during the first day of the green corn ceremony or busk when the warriors cleaned the busk ground, sprinkled fresh white sand over the area, and lighted the first busk fire.[6] At Kasita, according to Hawkins, it was used again on the fifth day when the second busk fire was laid. As the second sequence of four days of the busk was in many respects a duplication of the first four days, each use of black drink seems to have been part of the preparatory cleansing ritual of the busk. During the eighth day of the busk, a mixture of up to fourteen herbal teas was prepared and taken as the climax of the busk ceremony, but *Ilex vomitoria* was not part of this mixture.

A description of the busk given to Swan by Anthony Alexander McGillivray indicates that black drink played an important role in the busk and perhaps in the scheduling of the event:

When the corn is ripe, and the cassine or new black drink has come to perfection, the busking begins . . . four young men come forward in the same manner, each having a fair ear of new corn, which the priest takes from them, and places with great solemnity on the fire, where is is consumed. Four young warriors then enter the square in the manner mentioned, each having some of the new cassena. A small part of it is given to the new fire by the priest, and the remainder is immediately parched and cooked for use.[7]

Ilex vomitoria leaves were thus offered to the new fire of the busk in the same manner as corn, and it therefore participates with cultivated vegetables in the first fruits ceremonial aspect of the busk. To what extent the maturing of *Ilex vomitoria* served as an element in the scheduling of the busk is far from clear. Certainly the primary concern in the time of the ceremony was the maturing of the corn to the stage when the kernels were filled with milk. In past ages, beans were probably also given a first fruits ceremony, but *Ilex vomitoria* seems to have been the only non-food plant so treated. That the offering of cassina to the new fire was made after the corn was offered indicates the *Ilex* leaves were not being offered as a preliminary to the corn oblation but as a subsidiary element. The fact that the busk was scheduled anywhere from late June to early August, depending on the ripening of the first corn crop, would indicate that *Ilex vomitoria* was considered ripe at that time. *Ilex vomitoria* sends out new shoots and leaves early in the summer but will continue to leaf if pruned throughout the growing season.

Black drink was used daily to purify and strengthen social ties. It is this daily or frequent use of black drink that was perhaps most important to the Creeks. According to the Chekilli migration legend, it was given by the Palachuclas (Apalachicolas) to the Cussitaws (Kasitas) to convert them from warlike ways to peaceful ones.[8] When General Oglethorpe visited the Creek towns on the lower Chattahoochee in the summer of 1739, he was preparing for a treaty with the Lower Creeks as part of his plans for war with the Spanish in Florida. A ranger who accompanied Oglethorpe described their reception in Coweta as beginning when the party was camped about two miles from the town. The Indians brought food of various kinds from Coweta and gave it to the English; at mid-morning, after they had eaten, they set out for the town. Met at the edge of the town by the chiefs and warriors, they were ceremoniously led to prepared seats, evidently in the town square. Here they were given "black drink in Conkshells which they presented to us and as we were drinking they kept Hooping and Hallowing as a token of gladness in seeing us."[9]

Black drink, along with tobacco, seems to have been regularly offered to important persons visiting in Creek towns. David Taitt visited widely among the Upper and Lower Creeks during 1772 as part of a general peace-seeking and spying mission for the superintendent of Indian affairs, John Stuart. Because he had also been instructed to prepare a map of the Creek country, he traveled widely, and many of his visits were to towns where he did not plan to prepare for peace discussions. On the first morning of his visit to a particular town, he usually was offered tobacco and black drink in the town square. On subsequent visits during his stay, he would usually resort to the square or to the council house, depending on the weather and season, for tobacco and black drink. Taitt's journal indicates that the leading men and chiefs of the town were generally in the square or council house in the morning and that black drink was taken before breakfast or before any discussions. On several occasions, when Taitt wanted a more formal discussion, he mentions the black drink ceremony in the evening, often for the second time within one day.[10]

On several occasions Taitt mentions that the men "were at black in the square" in terms that make it clear that this was a habitual practice. The ceremony of drinking black drink and smoking tobacco usually was concluded at about ten in the morning, when Taitt and the Indians proceeded to their own affairs, including breakfast. Taitt usually links the drinking of black drink in the town square or council house with the exchange of tobacco, or at least the general smoking of tobacco, both actions seeming to be a general pattern of fellowship, preparation for the day, and restrained good relationships. He was offered black drink from February 14, 1772 onward through May. During the later part of his trip he visited the Lower Creek towns along the middle Chattahoochee. During this period he less frequently mentions a black drink ceremony in the village square.

When Taitt arrived in Chiaha on April 29 he was given black drink in the square. Later that day he held a conference at Kasita, across the river. A cohorn cannon was fired to welcome him and his visit seems to have been well received, and although he records that he smoked tobacco with the chiefs, he does not mention black drink.[11] I get the distinct impression that while smoking tobacco was a regular feature of daily town square activity, black drink was taken somewhat irregularly, at least among the Chattahoochee towns of the Lower Creeks at this particular time. During the period of Taitt's visit, relationships between the Lower Creek towns and the English were somewhat strained, which may explain the omission of the black drink ceremony. On every occasion when Taitt talked in public to the assembled chiefs, however, both black drink and tobacco were used in opening ceremonies for the talks.

The Quaker botanist William Bartram mentions the use of black drink as occurring both in the morning and in the evening. He describes rather elaborate preparations for drinking black drink at Attassee on the upper Tallapposa River in central Alabama during the winter of 1775/76.[12] In its general use black drink seems to have been customarily accompanied with the smoking of tobacco. Caleb Swan observed that "a stranger going among them cannot recommend himself to their protection in any manner so well as by offering to partake of it with them as often as possible." [13]

The most frequent use, then, of black drink was to cement friendship and promote communication, either within the town square in warm weather or inside the council house during the winter. It was used to promote easy interchange among the Indians themselves and between the Indians and visiting whites. To smoke tobacco and to drink caffeineated beverages is even today in many parts of the world a sign of interpersonal accommodation. This use to promote peaceable communication and social ease may well have been the role it played in the great ceremonials such as the busk, where it seems to have been used principally at the beginning of the rituals, especially on the most important days. Moreover, it seems to have been accepted by Europeans as a regular part of doing business with the Creeks, and other southeastern Indians.

All early writers agree that black drink was made from the leaves of *Ilex vomitoria,* and, since it is a coastal plant, its widespread use in the interior must have presented some procurement problems.[14] While most early writers emphasize that *Ilex vomitoria* was especially characteristic of the coastal zones, none of the early observers of the Creeks mention trade in cassina between that group and coastal tribes, although the coastal Indians did trade with unspecified western Indians. Bartram specifically mentions a transplanted stand of *Ilex vomitoria* at Jore in the Cherokee country of North Carolina,[15] but nowhere else does he mention it as a cultivated plant among the southern Indians. Adair implies that it was transplanted to inland sites: "There is a species of tea, that grows spontaneously, and in great plenty, along the sea-coast of the two Carolinas, Georgia, and East and West Florida, which we call *Yopon,* or *Cusseena:* the Indians transplant, and are extremely fond of it; they drink it on certain stated occasions."[16]

Hawkins is the only author who mentions *Ilex vomitoria* at specific Creek towns, saying there were clumps of "youpon" growing at "Took-au-bat-che" and "Oc-fus-kee." Both these towns were well inland in Alabama, at or above the fall line.

Swan, in a very complete discussion of black drink, simply says that the Indians collected, parched, and boiled it.[17] I get the impression from the numerous discussions of the preparation and use of black drink that the leaves were generally picked and parched immediately before making the tea. This would suggest that either scattered natural stands of *Ilex vomitoria* existed on the lower Piedmont or that the Creeks maintained cultivated plots of the bush.

At present the natural range of *Ilex vomitoria* has been extended because of its use as an ornamental shrub. Hedges of *Ilex vomitoria* are fairly common in central Georgia, along the lower Piedmont. In 1940 a number of plants three feet high were taken from Fort Pulaski National Monument and transplanted at Ocmulgee, at Macon, Georgia. Here, planted in stiff clay soil, they grew very successfully. None of these plants, originally growing in salty sand on the coast, died in the transplanting process. Although they were transported in trucks at a much more rapid rate than would have been possible for the Creeks, it still seems that they withstand transplating well and readily acclimate to upland soils. More than thirty years later the plants at Ocmulgee are still healthy; some, unpruned, have grown to a height of about twelve feet. They regularly produce berries and appear to be thoroughly at home. The berries are eaten by migratory birds, especially the cedar waxwing, usually on their northward migration in early spring. The birds can be presumed to have spread the plant in the vicinity. Occasionally *Ilex vomitoria* plants are found in an apparently wild state in the lower Piedmont, but this cannot of itself be taken as an indication of its aboriginal range because of the widespread modern use of yaupon as an ornamental plant. It is plain, however, that *Ilex vomitoria* could be transplanted rather easily by any people even roughly familiar with agriculture.

While estimates of the amount of yaupon leaves used by the Creeks are set about with so many variables that cannot be quantified accurately, even a rough calculation may throw some light on our problems. As a minimum amount we might assume that only Tukabachee used it every day and that the other fifty or more Creek towns used it on the average of twice a week. Again, assuming a minimum of ten men in the square, each taking about one quart three or four times at each meeting, we would come up with 885 brewings. One cup of parched yaupon leaves, strongly boiled, will yield about one quart of tea. This means that a town's minimal yearly consumption of *Ilex vomitoria* leaves would be on the order of 550 bushels of leaves, or 27 cubic yards, the equivalent of 10 sizeable truckloads. If we should assume that most Creek towns used the same amounts daily, as seems highly likely, we come out with considerably larger figures. The total consumption would then be nearly 600 cubic yards, which would have entailed either a caravan of large trucks from the coast or an aboriginal bucket brigade. I find it hard to believe that such a trade from the coast, even at minimal consumption, could have existed during the eighteenth century without being remarked upon by a contemporary observer. In view of the ready acclimization of *Ilex vomitoria* to the Piedmont, it might be suggested that the intensive use by the Creeks may have virtually exterminated aboriginal stands. As the Creeks became more involved in trade with Europeans, perhaps they neglected local stands and over-pruned existing specimens to such an extent that the once natural stands in the interior were extinguished.

Certainly the large quantities of yaupon leaves used by the Creeks in the interior required either considerable local supplies or a well-developed trade system. So far as I know, the presence of *Ilex vomitoria* has not been demonstrated for any Creek site by either archeological remains or by pollen analysis. It seems clear then that it was almost certainly transplanted and maintained in the interior. This may well be the only case of cultivation of a woody plant in the aboriginal Southeast; all the usual Creek agricultural plants are annuals. It implies a sophistication in agriculture which well agrees with the heavy dependence of the Creeks on plant cultivation.

After the leaves, and perhaps the tender stems, had been collected, they were lightly toasted in clay basins or pans over the fire. Romans says that both the toasting and the brewing were done by the women, while other authors are silent.[18] The parching of the leaves makes the caffeine more soluble and was recognized by several colonial writers as being similar to the roasting of coffee and tea. In trying this with freshly picked *Ilex vomitoria* leaves, I found that the leaves are parched to a chocolate brown in a moderately warm skillet in two or three minutes. Some stirring is helpful to prevent drier leaves from burning. It is probable that the Indians toasted fairly large quantities of leaves in earthen pots, and this would have taken somewhat longer than in the iron skillets I used. In my experience it is difficult to toast naturally dried leaves because they tend to ignite, the whole mass bursting into flame. Milfort says that "its leaf is gathered only when it is to be served."[19] The toasting process releases aromatic oils that have a pleasant spicy aroma. It was apparently the only Creek medicine that was toasted before being brewed.

Once toasted, the Indians steeped or boiled the leaves in earthen pots to brew the tea. Apparently the parched leaves could be stored for some time with little deterioration. Most of the early accounts, however, indicate that fresh leaves were toasted and immediately boiled. I am under the impression that parched *Ilex vomitoria* leaves require more boiling to produce a standard tea than does oriental tea. Simply steeping the leaves in boiling water produces a very weak pale tea. Most early accounts describe black drink as being boiled until it was very dark, hence the common name for it among the whites. Gatschet, writing in the nineteenth century, says that it was made in three graduated strengths.[20]

After the leaves had been boiled they were removed from the tea by pouring it through a strainer made of split cane.[21] This probably was a special basketry utensil used for the sacred tea, but it was most likely made in a manner similar to the sifters used in the preparation of corn meal. After it was strained, the tea was either poured from one pot to another[22] or back and forth from a pot into gourds.[23] In this process a white froth formed on top often compared to the foam on beer or ale. Several Europeans of the period thought that it had been fermented, but there was too little time for fermentation to have taken place, and black drink clearly was not an alcoholic beverage. Swan says that this froth gave it the name among the Indians of "white drink," although he also recognizes that the purifying qualities ascribed to it would have qualified it for the designation of "white."[24]

Unlike the other great teas of the Creeks, supernatural power was not blown into black drink. During the preparation of the other three major drinks a priest blew his breath through a cane into the brew, thus imparting his thoughts and spiritual power into the tea. This was not done with cassina, the tea apparently having its own inherent power to resolve differences and promote peace.

The brewing, and probably the gathering, of *Ilex vomitoria* was under the direction of the second chiefs, or *Henihalgi,* who were charged with overseeing public works, work in the town fields, along with supervising the making and serving of black drink. These men, usually one or two in each town with a square, were men of permanent position, next in rank to the Micco, or town chief. Within the towns they were chosen from "white" or peace clans.[25] Sitting beside the Micco at councils and public assemblies, they were men of considerable influence and completely dedicated to peace.

Descriptions differ concerning where the actual preparation of black drink took place. Swan says that it was prepared over a fire in the center of the square.[26] Bartram is equally positive that it took place in "an open shed or pavilion, at twenty or thirty yards distance, directly opposite the door of the council-house,"[27] but because he was describing the situation at the Attassee hot house, he might actually be referring to one of the cabins or arbors of the square. If the tea were brewed in the square or its immediate vicinity, it seems unlikely that women would have been the preparators, for most activities of the square were closed to women. Wherever it was prepared, it was drunk very warm, or hot. The boiling process and dark color would indicate a brew with a high caffeine content, which, as a hot liquid, would have been assimilated readily by those who drank it.

Once brewed, black drink was served by special persons in a highly ritualized manner. One specially designated person, or in some accounts two such persons, served it to the accompaniment of a long singing note. In some accounts[28] these servers are described as old or mature men; in others they are said to be young men.[29] The existence of these servers points up the importance and ritual character of black drink. They are mentioned in nearly all the accounts written during the eighteenth century, strongly suggesting that black drink was never drunk casually, even when taken daily.

Black drink was served in special cups or bowls of rather large capacity. Adair, Bartram, the ranger with Oglethorpe, and one of Swanton's informants say that these cups were conch shells (see fig. 9).[30] Swan, Stiggins, Taitt, General Dale, Bossu, and Milfort say that black drink was served in gourds or "calabashes."[31] Swanton's informant and Adair are quite specific in saying that the conch shell cups or dippers were regarded as semi-sacred. As Jerald Milanich has indicated in the preceding chapter, the association of the conch shell cup with black drink seems sufficiently strong to serve as evidence of the use of the tea.

A drawing of one of the beds or cabins comprising the Alabama town square in the early eighteenth century is shown in figure 11. The cabin opens in front with two tiers of seats.

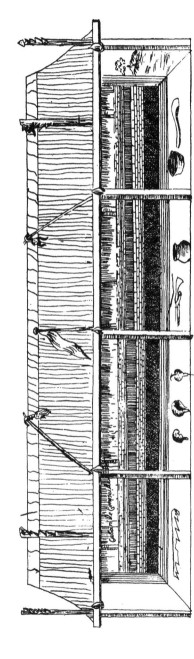

Figure 11. Cabin on the Alabama town square. Courtesy of the Smithsonian Institution, National Anthropological Archives, negative no. 1169-B-1.

Under the roof in front are two medicine pots and a long wooden spoon. In the second section, on the cabin's right side (to the left of the viewer), are three objects which appear to be a conch shell cup in the center and additional shell cups on each side, or perhaps gourds. A musket and a notched war club (*atasa*) lie on the floor. The roof is decorated with flags and additional *atasa*. Since there is no suggestion of a fire for brewing the tea, this apparently shows the equipment for taking black drink but not for preparing it.[32]

In the serving ritual, the servers offered the cup, containing upward of a quart of hot tea, to the principal chief first, then in strict declining order to each person present. The rank of each drinker was thus frequently verified in public by the position of his seat in the council house or square, and by the order in which he was served black drink. While each man was drinking, the server sang a long musical note, usually transcribed as "Yahola." The recipient had to keep drinking, or at least hold the cup to his mouth, while this note was being sung.[33] Yahola was one of a pair of male deities who lived in the sky and who were regarded as perfect, clean, and undefiled. Thus the Yahola cry was in a sense an invocation of these qualities on the drinker in accord with the function of black drink as a cleansing agent.[34] Several writers suggest that the servers sang an additional song as they approached the chief with the drink.[35]

All persons who described the used of black drink in the town squares on an almost daily basis mention this elaborate ritualized custom in connection with the tea. It is true that many travelers simply said that "they took black drink" or that they "went to the square for black drink," but there is no evidence of both a ritualized and a secular manner of drinking. This black drink ritual was, apparently, generally accompanied by the sharing of tobacco. On occasion when visitors were being welcomed to a town, the pipes and tobacco pouches were elaborately presented and passed from man to man, evidently again in order of rank. The smoking of tobacco in pipes, symbolizing peace, was generally the opening act of negotiations among

American Indians. It seems to have very largely functioned as a gesture of friendliness. Thus the use of black drink and tobacco in the village squares on an almost daily basis by the men of the town, especially the chiefs and elders, along with the manner in which they were taken, may be seen as a rather stylized ritual of friendship, fellowship, and togetherness. Stiggins speculated that the custom "originated through political motives, viz., for the purpose of assembling the towns people frequently at their town house or square in order to keep them united."[36]

A war name, *Asi Yahola,* or "Black Drink Singer," was used among the Creeks. This name was held by the famous Seminole Osceola, who was born among the Upper Creeks in Alabama, later moving while still a child to Florida.[37] It is not clear whether this ceremonial title *Asi Yahola* was given to the servers of black drink or whether it was a separate title. As we have already seen, some accounts say that the servers were young men, others say that they were mature or older men. This strongly suggests that the position of black drink server was a regularly constituted position in the hierarchy of Creek chiefs. Thus some travelers would have seen young recently appointed servers, while other visitors at a later date or in another town might have seen men who had held the position for some time. Adair is the authority for the statement that the "consecrated conchshells" were in the custody of a priest,[38] evidently a Heniha. Certainly the serving of black drink was surrounded with considerable ritual, especially the invocation of the protection of supernatural beings. Adair states that

There is a carved human statue of wood, to which, however, they pay no religious homage. It belongs to the head war town of the upper Muskohge country, and seems to have been originally designed to perpetuate the memory of some distinguished hero, who deserved well of his country; for when their *cusseena,* or bitter, Black Drink is about to be drank in the synhedrion, they frequently, on common occasions, will bring it there, and honour it with the first conch-shell full, by the hand of the chief religious attendant: and then they return it to its former place. It is observable that the same beloved waiter, or holy attendant, and his coadjutant, equally observe the same ceremony to every person of reputed merit, in that quadrangular place [39]

Adair is also the authority for the statement that peace negotiations were opened by the drinking of black drink and the smoking of tobacco.[40] On occasions when treaty negotiations were conducted away from regularly constituted towns, the Creek delegation seems to have built their camp with a square where black drink was taken before discussions.[41]

After the Indians took black drink they sometimes regurgitated it. Opinions of observers differ on just how strong an emetic black drink may have been. Swan says that it was a gentle diuretic and does not seem to have regarded it as strongly emetic.

It is generally served round in this manner three times at every meeting; during the recess of serving it up, they all sit quietly in their several cabins, and amuse themselves by smiling, conversing, exchanging tobacco, etc., and in disgorging what black-drink they have previously swallowed.

Their mode of disgorging, or spouting out the black-drink, is singular, and has not the most agreeable appearance. After drinking copiously, the warrior, by hugging his arms across his stomach, and leaning forward, disgorges the liquor in a large stream from his mouth, to the distance of six or eight feet. Thus, immediately after drinking, they begin spouting on all sides of the square, and in every direction; and in that country, as in others more civilized, it is thought a handsome accomplishment in a young fellow to be able to spout well.[42]

Evidently Swan did not feel that the drink was a violent emetic, but that the vomiting needed some assistance, such as hugging the stomach. Stiggins remarks:

It is singular how this tea operates on them after they drink it, for after they have drunk it they retain it in their stomachs for near a half hour. They can discharge their stomach of it as often as they drink it, with seeming ease, spouting it out of their mouths as it were by eruction. After four or five drinks and discharges of their stomach at different times of near a quart at a time, the black drink being over they disperse at or near ten o'clock; it acts as a tonic, as it is drunk of a morning fasting.[43]

Clairborne says that they retained it for about fifteen minutes and vomited without any effort or artificial means.[44] Bossu notes that "they throw it up without any effort and without inconvenience."[45] None of these authors seem to have been concerned with an accurate assessment of the emetic properties. Perhaps the most specific account is given by the French adventurer Milfort, who in describing his first visit to the Creek Nation relates his experiences at the national assembly.

Although I was absolutely ignorant of the significance of such a ceremony and the nature of the beverage that was being offered me, I did not venture to show any distrust and tried it. Finding that it tasted like tea without sugar, I drank a considerable quantity of it. Shortly after the entire assembly had partaken of this beverage, I noticed that the Indians vomited it very easily and without the slightest effort. This spectacle, which by the way was exceedingly disgusting, made me a little uneasy, and I began to fear that it was medicine and that I had no doubt taken by far too large a dose. McGillivray, noting my amazement, asked me in English why I did not follow suit. I replied that, as yet, I felt no inclination to vomit, that very likely the physic would operate in a much more natural way.[46]

Milfort goes on to conclude that the purpose of black drink was to assure the chiefs that the councils were carried out with empty stomachs and presumably free of the influence of alcoholic drinks.

David Taitt, who traveled in the Upper and Lower Creek country from February 14 to May 26, 1776, states that he took black drink on at least thirty occasions. While he is often quite specific about what he was given to eat, the weather, and so on, he never mentions that he was discomfited by the black drink.[47] Apparently, Europeans were not expected to disgorge black drink, and none of them describe it as a violent emetic.

The *Ilex vomitoria* leaves I have brewed produced a pleasant slightly aromatic tea, which I have generally drunk slightly weaker than is described for the Creeks. Although thoroughly aware of the reputation, and of the Latin name, of the drink, at no time have I felt any stomach distress. If drunk warm, a slightly astringent tea might be easy to disgorge, but I do not believe that its importance among the Creeks depended basically on its emetic effect. I believe the "purifying" designation was due to the stimulating effect of the caffeine that it contained. Drunk hot, a strong brew of *Ilex vomitoria* does result in the pick-up effect noted by most users of caffeine. Perhaps the fifteen to thirty minutes that the drink was retained, along with the rather copious quantities drunk, would have been sufficient for much of the caffeine to have been absorbed. The war medicine or *Pasa,* made of button snakeroot, was a rather violent emetic, and it was evidently this to which Milfort referred when he said that it made him violently sick when he was being inducted as a Great Tastanagi or War Chief.[48]

Black drink seems to have been drunk only by adult men among the Creeks, never by women or children. It thus served as an identification of adult male status in a society otherwise strongly emphasizing female power and authority. The Creeks, as well as most of the other southeastern tribes, were strongly matrilineal and matrilocal. A person remained a member of his mother's clan throughout his life, and many Creek positions of authority were tied to specific matrilineal clans. They were, in effect, inherited through the female line, although the most able member of the clan was usually selected to fill the office to which that clan was entitled.[40] Certainly black drink, taken by the adult men of the town either in the hot house in winter or the square in summer, was widely regarded as conferring social accommodation, friendship, peace, and benevolence on the assembled men of the town. The emetic action that was interpreted as having a cleansing effect must have been secondary. Its ancient nature and thorough integration into Creek town life seems to mean that its major function was not its possible sobering effect, as suggested by Milfort, because it must long antedate the appearance of alcohol among the southern Indians.

The use of black drink spans a long period in Creek history and evidently has a much longer unrecorded existence if we consider the thorough way in which it was integrated into Creek town life. The use of black drink is mentioned in the Chikili migration legend given to Oglethorpe at Savannah in 1735.[50] The earliest description of its use seems to be that given in the account of Oglethorpe's trip to Coweta and Kasita on the Chattahoochee River in 1739.[51] During the entire eighteenth century it is frequently mentioned as a regular feature of daily, or nearly daily, meetings of the town chiefs and elders in the town square or the hot house. With the removal to the Indian Territory early in the nineteenth century, it became much more difficult to procure the leaves, and the beverage gradually dropped from use, although it was remembered as one of the four sacred medicines as late as the early twentieth century, when John R. Swanton collected information from Creeks in Oklahoma.[52] The general disorganization resulting from this enforced migration and the attendant readaptation to quite different conditions may have been a major factor in the loss of black drink rituals from Creek culture in the nineteenth century.

Among the Seminoles of Florida, an off-shoot of the main body of the Creeks, the use of black drink seems to parallel rather closely its use among the parent body. The Seminoles were constituted out of Creek towns and individuals who voluntarily moved into Florida following the destruction of the aboriginal peninsular population by Carolina slavers early in the eighteenth century.[53] This movement was augmented after the Creek War of 1814 by numerous refugees from the revitalizationist faction among the Upper Creeks. During the period from about 1720, when Creeks began to arrive in Florida, until the 1760s, when the Florida bands had begun to be distinguishable from their kinsmen in Georgia and Alabama, they made many adjustments to the new environment and to new external relationships.

Bartram describes the use of black drink at the conclusion of a feast given for the white traders and himself in the Seminole town of Talahasochte, on the lower Suwanee River in Levy County, Florida in 1774.[54] On this occasion black drink was taken after a feast and after tobacco had been passed around. Thus its use differed somewhat from the usual morning ritual. Since the taking of black drink by the Seminole on this occasion preceded immediately the ratification of a trading treaty recently concluded at St. Augustine, it did in fact conform to the peacemaking pattern of its use. A short time later, at another Seminole town of Cuscowilla, treaty discussions were held before, rather than after, a feast.

The Florida Seminole today still retain a word for black drink, but they no longer use *Ilex vomitoria*. Instead they brew two "black drinks," one from button snakeroot, the other from willow bark, corresponding to the *pasa* and *miko hoyanidja* of the earlier Creeks. They are used on Court Day of the annual busk, the same day in which men and boys are scratched as in the old days. These two teas are brewed, probably much in the old way, and spiritual power is blown into them by a medicine man. A number of factors seem to be involved in the changes found among the Seminole. The name that they now use for *miko hoyanidja* is *ac-wa-nah* (medicine water). It apparently contains the root *wa-nah* for medicine, perhaps, and a modifier *ac*, which may represent the older name for water. *Ilex vomitoria* is probably not found in the Everglades, the present home of the Florida Seminoles.[55] It does occur, however, somewhat to the north of their area and certainly within fairly easy access. What have been retained are only two, perhaps originally the most important, of the four sacred medicines. None of the daily ritual of drinking black drink to promote friendship and good feelings remains. The modern Florida Seminole, living in small lineage camps and increasingly involved in the affairs of white Florida, perhaps do not feel the need for ritual to heighten cohesion. The fact that they have moved out of the natural range of *Ilex vomitoria* may have contributed to the disuse of the ancient drink.

Obviously black drink played an important role in the daily lives of Creek men. This fundamental function of giving the

men a focal point of companionship and interaction was strongly related to the roles that men played in the society. Cohesion
among all the men of a town was important in deciding affairs
of war and peace, in organizing for the great ceremonials, and
probably in hunting activities as well. Most of the protein
in their diet was derived from the men's hunting activities.
Creek society was largely structured around the matrilineal
families and matrineal clans. Some device for promoting cohesion among men was needed if the men were to perform their
duties satisfactorily in the society as a whole. It is probable that
some exclusively male-centered daily activity was necessary to
maintain male solidarity between the sporadic occasions when
men had to act in concert. Black drink, along with the sharing
of tobacco, seems to have filled this need admirably. Almost
universally early travelers report that black drink was regarded
as promoting benevolence, friendship, and peace within the
town and with visitors.

The importance of black drink was signalized for the Creeks
by the fact that the *Henihalgi* chiefs supervised its preparation,
by the ritual way in which it was served, by the invocation of
a deity *Yahola* while serving it, and by the existence of an hon-
orary war title, *Asi Yohola*. Its importance was further symbolized for the Creeks by the blessing of the *Ilex vomitoria* at
the new fire of the busk ceremony, along with the major food
staple, corn. I suspect that the disgorging of black drink, not
in itself a strong emetic, may have served to connect it with the
major ceremonial medicines, of which *pasa* or button snakeroot seems to be the most powerful emetic and physic. Certainly *Ilex vomitoria* tea does not in itself seem to produce this
effect, because no European travelers mention that they themselves were inconvenienced by drinking it. It was always the
Indians who vomited, perhaps as a learned social skill.

If we look for parallels with black drink and tobacco in our
society we see that the morning-coffee-and-cigarette syndrome
of the suburban housewife resembles the black drink ritual in
a number of ways. It is certainly prevalent among a group
which does not participate directly in the organized activities

(business) of the society. It offers, along with the habitual use of tobacco and the cerebral stimulation of caffeine, an opportunity to catch up on recent events of social import, and an occasion for planning the day's campaigns. Surely a good slug of caffeine does promote a feeling of euphoria, benevolence, and cooperation. In the case of our own society, the custom of the morning coffee break (often, until the intervention of the surgeon general, combined with tobacco) has spread to industry as an institutionalized ritual. The organization of a coffee lounge is followed immediately by a rising sense of moral solidarity and a lessening of internal division.

In our consideration of black drink in the Southeast, one can raise the question of why it never became an integral element of southern culture. Certainly early settlers had ample opportunities to observe its use. Coffee and tea were caffeine stimulants already present in the culture, and there was a rather conscious search for resources in the New World which could be procured locally rather than being imported. Of course, cassina or yaupon tea did enter southern culture to some extent, but it did not win a permanent place in the culture. It could be argued that the spectacle of Indians enthusiastically disgorging the tea would not recommend it to strangers. Nevertheless, it was adopted. It simply never became popular. Perhaps a brief look at the course to popularity of another caffeine drink in the South would offer some clues about what makes for successful adoption. I specifically refer to the rise of the cola drinks in the South, especially Coca-Cola.

The history of Coca-Cola begins with the American Civil War and the innovation of one of its most famous cavalry generals, Thomas Jonathan Jackson. Jackson acquired the name "Stonewall" at the first battle of Manassas, called Bull Run by Northern historians. While he may have valiantly stood with his Virginians like a stone wall on the ridge above Bull Run, his major contribution to military tactics was his perfection of the use of cavalry. He, along with other Southern cavalry leaders, perfected the techniques of the rapid raid to cut enemy supply lines, gather information in the enemy's rear, and strike from the deep flank. Much of "Stonewall" Jackson's success was due to his use of the ten-minute break. He rode his men for fifty minutes, rested them for ten, to arrive at his objective fresher and more frequently victorious.

The War between the States, like all major conflicts, had its full share of military observers from other nations. These observers noticed four major innovations: the use of railroads to move troops and supplies, the use of trench warfare, the use of rifled artillery, and the use of the ten-minute break. Busily reporting these developments, they introduced them into European armies of the time. By World War I the use of railroads, trenches, rifled artillery, and the ten-minute break were common in all western armies. The mechanical aspects of rifled cannon and rail transport of troops or supplies had been tremendously elaborated in an increasingly technological culture. Southern cavalry tactics had been refined in our own Indian wars, with occasional disasters at such places as the Little Big Horn. The general pattern of hit-and-run cavalry raids had undergone extensive elaboration, first in Homer Lea's military teaching in China, and finally in the lightning strikes of the German armor on the Western Front in 1940. Trench warfare seems to have reached its peak during World War I but became obsolete with the development of wars of movement on land and in the air. The ten-minute break shows an even more complex evolution and is perhaps the only one of these innovations to enter civilian peacetime culture.

When the French adopted the ten-minute break, they found it necessary to modify it to facilitate its acceptance into French military culture. With fine French logic they added a drink to the break period. At first this was simply sugar, water, color, and flavoring. At about the same time the Corsican Angelo Mariani had begun to market "Vin Coca Mariani," a simple elixir of coca leaves in sherry wine. Widely popular, Vin Coca Mariani seems to have been joined to the French ten-minute break drink as a welcome stimulant and pick-me-up. Later when the French began to expand their colonial holdings in North Africa, they recruited large numbers of Sudanese troops, mainly as labor battalions. These people were addicted to the use of the cola nut, *Cola nitida,* which contains slight amounts of caffeine and a glucoside, kolanin. Its effect is to produce stimulation, greater physical ability, and a lessening of hunger and fatigue.[56] Cola, or simple extractions of the nut, was added to Vin Mariani, and the ten-minute break was augmented again to make it acceptable in still another culture.

Crossing the Atlantic, the ten-minute break next appears in the form of Coca-Cola syrup developed in 1886 by John S. Pemberton, an Atlanta pharmacist. Intended to be mixed with carbonated water at the soda fountain, the syrup contained the familiar sugar, color, flavoring, cola extractive, and the elixir of coca leaves from Vin Coca Mariani. Carbonated beverages were widely popular in America at the time, and many druggists were mixing their own formulas. The exact ingredients of Coca-Cola remain secret to this day; we therefore cannot be sure what the constituents are, but evidently caffeine and cola extract are among them. Until the federal legislation controlling the distribution of narcotics, it seems likely that the "coca" element of the drink was derived from coca leaves.[57]

Asa Griggs Candler purchased the assets of the Pemberton drug firm in 1888 and eventually became the sole proprietor of the formula. Like many early entrepreneurs of soft drinks, Candler was an aggressive advertiser, setting a style that persists until the present. After 1894 Coca-Cola was bottled, leading to a proliferation of local distributors; it was no longer solely available at the drugstore soda fountain. In 1915 Alexander Samuelson, of the Root Glass Company of Terre Haute, Indiana designed the classic Coca-Cola bottle which was ready to receive a container patent, and which remains virtually unchanged to the present day.[58]

While the advertising slogans of Coca-Cola have changed with the times, as have the styles of the girls who usually are a prominent part of the displays, a recurrent theme has been "The Pause That Refreshes," a newer version of the ten-minute break originally devised by Stonewall Jackson. It would seem that the rest pause achieved cultural integration through the addition of Vin Coca Mariani in France, cola in North Africa, and carbonation, bottling, and advertising in the United States.

What is of interest is that the success of Coca-Cola, and a veritable host of imitators, demonstrates the place in the nineteenth- and twentieth-century American culture for a caffeine and sugar drink that could be widely and cheaply distributed. People in the South during this period were at least marginally familiar with cassina tea but did not adopt it. Perhaps its reputation as an emetic had something to do with its rejection. Items of Indian religious affiliation were not as easily adopted as were the basic subsistence items of corn, beans, and squash. The cultural milieu was wrong. Black drink was part of a religious complex that had very low prestige among the white settlers. It was used in town council situations, not as a part of daily meals or relaxation. It seems to have been marginally accepted in the superordinate white society, as witnessed in its local use along the coasts of the Carolinas and Georgia. During the War between the States it served as a locally available substitute for tea and coffee. In the generation after that war, it was once again the possession of a defeated and subordinate group and thus lacking prestige. Perhaps the ability and energy of an Asa Griggs Candler were the elements that were necessary to develop a pause that refreshes into an international institution.

At the time when Coca-Cola was adopted enthusiastically by the Anglo-American culture, carbonated drinks were reaching their first full acceptance. "Sodas" of various flavors were proliferating. The situation almost dictated a search for new flavors. The marginal adoption of cassina tea, mainly along the coasts of the South, in effect removed it from consideration. It was a local folk drink, not readily acceptable to the new urban classes of the South. I doubt that its earlier presence among southern Indians was generally known to the developers of new proprietary flavors. On the other hand, mysterious flavors, sources of caffeine, and new names that could be exploited by aggressive advertising were much in demand. The subjugation and removal of the great bulk of the southern Indians had left their culture in disrepute. Only the crops of major importance, corn, beans, and squash, would be adopted by the newly crystalizing culture of the South. The development of an international trade in tea and coffee had removed any need for a search for local substitutes. This is in sharp contrast with the situation in South America, where *yerba maté*, brewed from a similar holly, became a part of Spanish-American culture. It was not the imponderables of history that resulted in the virtual loss of black drink, but the orientation of the culture that became dominant.

NOTES

1. Lewis H. Larson, "Settlement Distribution During the Mississippi Period," Southeastern Archaeological Conference Bulletin no. 13 (1970), pp. 19–25.

2. Charles H. Fairbanks, "Some Problems of the Origin of Creek Pottery," *Florida Anthropologist* 11 (1958): 53–64.

3. Charles H. Fairbanks, *Archaeology of the Funeral Mound, Ocmulgee National Monument, Georgia*. Intro. by Frank M. Setzler. National Park Service Archaeological Research Series, no. 3 (Washington, D.C., 1956).

4. Charles H. Fairbanks, "The Macon Earthlodge," *American Antiquity* 12 (1946): 94–108.

5. Caleb Swan, "Position and State of Manners and Arts in the Creek, or Muskogee Nation in 1791," in Henry Rowe Schoolcraft's *Historical and Statistical Information Respecting the History, Condition, and Prospects of the Indian Tribes of the United States,* vol. 5 (Philadelphia, 1855), pp. 251–83.

6. Benjamin Hawkins, "A Sketch of the Creek Country, in 1798 and '99," *Georgia Historical Society Collections* vol. 3 (Savannah, 1848), pp. 77–78.

7. Swan, "Muskogee Nation," pp. 267–68.

8. Albert S. Gatschet, *A Migration Legend of the Creek Indians* (Philadelphia: D. G. Brinton, 1884), vol. 1, p. 250.

9. Anonymous, "A Ranger's Report of Travels with General Oglethorpe in Georgia and Florida, 1739–1742," in *Travels in the American Colonies,* ed. Newton D. Mereness (New York: MacMillan Co., 1916), p. 220.

10. David Taitt, "David Taitt's Journal of a Journey Through the

Creek Country, 1772," in *Travels in the American Colonies,* ed. Newton D. Mereness (New York: MacMillan Co., 1916), pp. 493–565.

11. Taitt, "Journal," pp. 549–50.

12. Francis Harper, ed., *The Travels of William Bartram,* naturalists edition (New Haven: Yale University Press, 1958), pp. 284–86.

13. Swan, "Muskogee Nation," p. 266.

14. Richard Evans Schultes, "The Correct Name of the Yaupon," Harvard University Botanical Museum Leaflets, vol. 3, no. 4 (Cambridge, 1950), pp. 97–105.

15. Harper, "Travels of William Bartram," p. 227.

16. Samuel Cole Williams, ed., *Adair's History of the American Indians* (Johnson City, Tenn.: Watauga Press, 1930), pp. 48–49.

17. Swan, "Muskogee Nation," pp. 266–67.

18. Bernard Romans, *A Concise Natural History of East and West Florida.* A facsimile reproduction of the 1775 edition. Intro. by Rembert W. Patrick (Gainesville: University of Florida Press, 1962), pp. 94–95.

19. Louis LeClerc de Milfort, *Memoir of a Cursory Glance of My Different Travels and My Sojourn in the Creek Nation,* trans. Geraldine de Courcy, ed. John Francis McDermott (Chicago: Lakeside Press, R. R. Donnelley and Sons, 1956), p. 139.

20. Albert S. Gatschet, *Tchikilli's Kasi'hta Legend in the Creek and Hitchiti Languages.* Transactions of the Academy of Science of St. Louis, vol. 5, no. 1 (1888), pp. 56–57.

21. Taitt, "Journal," pp. 502–3.

22. Swan, "Muskogee Nation," p. 266.

23. J. F. H. Clairborne, *Mississippi as a Province, Territory, and State,* vol. 1 (1880; rpt. ed., Baton Rouge: Louisiana State University Press, 1964), p. 491.

24. Swan, "Muskogee Nation," p. 266.

25. John R. Swanton, "Social Organization and Social Usages of the Indians of the Creek Confederacy," Bureau of American Ethnology Forty-second Annual Report (Washington, D.C., 1928), pp. 192–97.

26. Swan, "Muskogee Nation," p. 266.

27. Harper, "Travels of William Bartram," p. 284.

28. Williams, *Adair's History,* p. 49.

29. Swan, "Muskogee Nation," p. 267.

30. Williams, *Adair's History,* p. 49; Harper, *Travels of William Bartram,* pp. 85–86; "Ranger's Report," p. 220; Swanton, "Social Organization and Social Usages," p. 503.

31. Swan, "Muskogee Nation," p. 267; Stiggins, in Theron A. Nunez, Jr., "Creek Nativism and the Creek War of 1813–1814," *Ethnohistory* 5 (1958): 36; Taitt, "Journal," p. 502; General Dale, quoted in Clairborne, *Mississippi,* p. 491; Jean-Bernard Bossu, *Travels in*

the Interior of North America, 1751–1762, trans. and ed. Seymour Feiler (Norman: University of Oklahoma Press, 1962), p. 141; Milfort, *Travels*, p. 139.

32. Baron Marc de Villiers, "Documents concernant l'Histoire des Indiens," *Journal de la Societé des Américanistes de Paris* 15 (1922): 136.

33. Swan, "Muskogee Nation," p. 267.

34. Ibid.

35. Ibid.

36. Nunez, "Creek Nativism," p. 154.

37. Mark F. Boyd, "Asi Yaholo or Osceola," *Florida Historical Quarterly* 33 (1955): 250–51.

38. Williams, *Adair's History*, p. 49.

39. Ibid.

40. Ibid., p. 176.

41. *American State Papers. Documents, Legislative and Executive, of the Congress of the United States* (Washington, D.C., 1832–34), class 2, Indian Affairs, vol. 1, p. 73. At the negotiations for the Treaty of Rock Landing on the Oconee River, September 24, 1789: "At the time appointed, the commissioners attended the ceremony of black drink, and were conducted to the great square of the encampment by all the kings, chiefs, and warriors, in solemn pomp, and much apparent friendship."

42. Swan, "Muskogee Nation," pp. 166–67.

43. Nunez, "Creek Nativism," p. 36.

44. Clairborne, *Mississippi,* 1:491.

45. Bossu, *Travels*, p. 141.

46. Milfort, *Memoir*, p. 141n9.

47. Taitt, "Journal," pp. 493–565.

48. Milfort, *Memoir*, p. 140.

49. Swanton, "Social Organization," pp. 192–97.

50. Gatschet, *A Migration Legend*, p. 350.

51. "Ranger's Report," p. 200.

52. John R. Swanton, "Religious Beliefs and Medical Practices of the Creek Indians." Bureau of American Ethnology Forty-second Annual Report (Washington, D.C., 1928), pp. 543–44.

53. Charles H. Fairbanks, "Ethnohistorical Report of the Florida Indians," in *Florida Indians III* (New York: Garland Publishing Co., 1974). This is the most complete source for the origin of the Seminole Nation.

54. Harper, *Travels of William Bartram*, p. 149.

55. Louis Capron, "The Medicine Bundles of the Florida Seminole and the Green Corn Dance," Smithsonian Institution, Bureau of American Ethnology Anthropological Papers, no. 35, Bulletin no. 151 (Washington, D.C., 1953).

56. O. Graff, "Zur Frage der spezifischen Wirkung der Cola auf die körperliche Leistungsfähigkeit," *Arbeitsphysiologie* 10 (1939): 376–95.

57. For the origins of Coca-Cola the best sources are: Charles Howard Candler, *Asa Griggs Candler* (Atlanta, Ga.: Emory University, 1950); this contains a general bibliography. The fiftieth anniversary issue of *The Coca-Cola Bottler,* vol. 51, no. 1 (April 1959), has a great deal of information. John J. Riley, *History of the Soft Drink Industry, Bottled Carbonated Beverages, 1807–1957* (Washington, D.C.: American Bottlers of Carbonated Beverages, 1958) discusses the complex as a whole. E. J. Kahn, *The Big Drink* (New York: Random House, 1960) is a journalistic story of Coca-Cola.

58. Craig Gilborn, "Poe Pedagory: Looking at the Coke Bottle," *Museum News,* December 1968, pp. 12–18 contains the best discussion of the persistence and evolution of the Coca-Cola bottle.

Black Drink and
Other Caffeine-containing Beverages
among Non-Indians

William C. Sturtevant

As was usual with many exotic beverages (and some foods) en-countered by Europeans, tea made from *Ilex vomitoria* was at first adopted or at least recommended for medicinal purposes, and only later did it become acceptable simply as food or stim-ulant. The Spaniards in St. Augustine, Florida (founded in 1565), adopted the drink from the nearby Timucua Indians and soon became addicted to it. In 1615 Father Ximénez char-acterized Spanish use of it with a remark familiar to any mod-ern American coffee drinker or British tea drinker: "any day that a Spaniard does not drink it, he feels that he is going to die." He reported that it was drunk first thing in the morning and that "there is no Spaniard or Indian who does not drink it every day in the morning and evening . . . it is more of a vice than chocolate in New Spain." But it was also highly valued as a strong diuretic, and it was believed to prevent urinary dis-eases. In fact, two Indians were sent from Florida to Spain specifically to prepare "cacina" to cure the Inquisitor Juan de Llanos de Valdes, canon of Seville, of such a disease. The In-dians, but evidently not the Spaniards, also used it as a purga-tive, adding a little sea water and purging themselves "very strongly above and below" (taken thus, it apparently served as an emetic as well as a purgative).

The same method of preparation was shared by Spaniards and Indians. Leaves were placed in a large hemispherical pot-tery vessel—historical archaeologists please note: a *cazuela*,

I am indebted to William L. Merrill for assistance in 1973 in research on these topics, and to Jacques Lafaye for a discussion of the recent uses of coffee, tea, and chocolate in France, Spain, and Mexico.

shaped like a *perol*—which was placed over a fire and stirred with a special stick until the leaves were toasted to a reddish color. Then, without removing the pot from the fire, water was gradually added until the pot was nearly full. After boiling, the leaves were removed, leaving a liquid the color of Spanish claret, with a foam on the surface "like that of chocolate when it is made with atole."[1]

This account is corroborated by a briefer report that in 1595 both Spaniards and Indians in St. Augustine drank "cacina" every morning. It was "the common drink of Spaniards and Indians," described as not bad tasting although not serving as a sweetmeat (*golosina*) as chocolate did elsewhere. Interestingly, the Spaniards were said to "have no memory of drinking sassafras except in illness." However, cassina itself was recognized as a diuretic, which was believed to prevent kidney stones.[2]

When Jonathan Dickinson, the Quaker castaway, and his party reached the Spanish posts on the coast below St. Augustine in 1696, they were offered local Spanish hospitality: "hot casseena drink" with maize bread or parched maize.[3] There is a report from 1701 from Santa María (probably on Amelia Island, Georgia) to the effect that the local Indians had defaulted on their obligation to deliver sixty *vices* (about two hundred pounds?) of "cazina" each month for the use of the small garrison of Spanish soldiers—who complained that they were forced to collect the leaves themselves.[4] For some years before 1725, according to another source, the only local products used by the Spanish families at St. Augustine (who were otherwise supplied from New Spain) were a little maize and "a drink, which they call Cacina, of which they use a lot."[5]

Well before this date English colonists were aware of this Indian drink and of its use by the Spaniards in Florida. Thomas Ashe, who was familiar with written accounts of "cassiny," was unable to learn of its use by local planters when he visited Charleston from 1680 to 1682. But he described it as a potentially useful Carolina plant in a pamphlet that he published in 1682.[6]

John Peachie, a Carolina physician, wrote to a friend in London in 1695 strongly recommending the use of *Ilex vomitoria* for treating smallpox.[7] He reported that he had often successfully prescribed a few drops of a tincture of "cassiny" administered in "water-gruel," "panado," a "posset-drink," "small beer," or "tare broath." Although he did not mention any other uses of *Ilex vomitoria* by local Europeans or by the Carolina Indians, he did give, in addition to his own experience, five references supporting the usefulness of the drink. He had heard that a few drops of cassiny from Carolina had been used successfully by a physician in London to treat smallpox (although perhaps at least as useful in effecting the cure was a live sheep kept constantly in the patient's room "to draw away the malignity," for the sheep died as the patient recovered). He reported that the virtues of the drink are mentioned in "an Account of Carolina" (probably that by Thomas Ashe); that Johannes De Laet's history of the West Indies describes it as a diuretic and a "Noble Beverage" used in Florida (in fact, De Laet[8] simply summarized Ximénez's description published in 1615); that Samuel Purchas mentions its use by Florida Indians in his *Pilgrimage* (the relevant passage[9] is a summary of Le Moyne's description of Timucua uses, published by De Bry [see Merrill's chapter in this volume]); and that "a famous Sea-Chyrurgeon" cured his passengers of smallpox with cassiny. So the implication is that Peachie was imitating Spanish uses, not local Indian ones, and the fact that he used the Florida name for the plant supports this supposition. But at the time Peachie wrote, published descriptions of the cacina plant itself were inadequate to have allowed it to be identified with the Carolina yaupon. The equation must have been made by someone who had seen the plant in both places or, less likely, by someone who had compared Carolina Indian (or inland Creek?) usages with those described for the Timucua. By 1695 Carolinian raids into Spanish Florida were well underway, and at least one prominent Carolinian had sufficient experience in Spanish St. Augustine and Guale to have made the identification: Dr. Henry Woodward, whose knowledge of Florida Spanish usage is illustrated by his reference to Creek chiefs as "Cassekas."[10]

However, the fact that the Carolinians later used the term *yaupon* (variously spelled) as well as the term *cassina* implies that they were familiar with their Indian neighbors' uses of the plant in addition to the Florida uses.

By the early eighteenth century *Ilex vomitoria* tea was widely used by whites, and presumably by blacks, in coastal North Carolina, and it is only here that the tea has continued in use up to the present day. Mark Catesby's classic description of *Ilex vomitoria*, based on observations between 1712 and 1725, includes the comment that "yapan" tea was much used by whites of coastal North Carolina.[11] Dr. John Brickell, writing in 1737 and plagiarizing Lawson for most of his account of "Yaupan, or Cassena," added some remarks regarding its use by non-Indians which were not in Lawson's account. Brickell included this "Indian tea" among the "Chocolate, Teas, and Coffee" which, he said, were as common in Carolina as in Ireland at that time and were beneficial as "sober Liquors" to which one became "addicted" in place of alcoholic drinks. This yaupon tea, "so very much in request amon[g]st both the Indians, and Christians," was used by the planters "with Physick," because of its "diuretick Quality," "by reason of it's safe and speedy passage through the Bowels and Ureters, which I have often experienced, and [it] is of excellent use in the Stone and Gravel." However, "it is likewise used as Tea, and in making Punch."[12] A fine description was published by the German traveler Johann David Schöpf, who visited North Carolina during 1783 and 1784 and reported that "yapan" tea, not China tea, was the customary breakfast drink in the coastal region. The tea was also used medicinally, and poor drinking water was purified by boiling it with a few yaupon leaves. To make tea, Schöpf said, careless users chopped up twigs, wood, and bark with the leaves, but better housekeepers separated the leaves alone (gathered at any season), then dried them in an iron kettle over a slow fire, pounded them slightly in a mortar, let them dry a bit more, and kept them in glass bottles. A pound of prepared leaves was worth one to one-and-a-half Spanish dollars, and Schöpf was told that the leaves had formerly been exported to England at a half guinea a pound, until the trade was stopped to prevent competition with Chinese tea.[13]

Nineteenth-century accounts of yaupon tea continued to mention its medicinal uses and to refer to it as a common drink on the North Carolina coast: "a useful diaphoretic" (1837); a diuretic and a cure for diabetes, gout, and smallpox (1863); a cure for alcoholism (1872); and for unspecified medicinal purposes (1913).[14] The use of yaupon leaves in purifying brackish water is mentioned in 1847 and 1863.[15] But by the 1890s drinking yaupon tea was scorned as a rural habit: "yeopon-eaters" was a derogatory term used by coastal people against the whites of the Outer Banks, and the supporters of a Hatteras team at a ballgame with Kinnakeet (modern Avon) invented the successful jeer "Kinnakeeters, Yaupon eaters."[16]

In 1928 it was reported that yaupon tea, once widely used on the southern coast, had disappeared nearly everywhere except on Knott's Island (in North Carolina on the Virginia border) "where nearly every farmer has a patch of yaupon in his yard, and puts up a barrel or so of it every year. The twigs are usually gathered in spring, chopped up with the leaves, and dried by artificial heat, so rapidly that they are scorched. When wanted for use a handful or so is put in a tea-kettle, with water, left on the stove indefinitely, and the decoction poured out when called for."[17]

In the early 1920s the United States Department of Agriculture conducted experiments and trials to determine the commercial potential of cassina, but the results were discouraging because of the competition of established coffee and tea habits. Toward the end of World War II the U.S.D.A. summarized its earlier work in a new circular, suggesting that cassina might be used during the coffee and tea shortage that then existed. Evidently the report came too late to be useful. This research began with knowledge of the continuing small-scale use of cassina tea in North Carolina (and Virginia), and with the recognition of the relatively high caffeine content of *Ilex vomitoria*, which was reported to average about the same as coffee but less than China tea. The use of leaf preparation techniques borrowed from Asian tea production resulted in the development of two types of cassina tea, green and black (the latter from slightly fermented leaves). About 420 gallons of hot cassina tea were served at the Charleston County Fair in 1922, and 5000 pounds of prepared leaves in half-pound packages were then tried on the market. Other experiments produced a cassina-flavored syrup, recommended for use in carbonated drinks and in or on ice cream. It was said to combine well with fruit and other flavors.[18] This, too, failed to catch on. If another attempt at commercial exploitation were to be made, it might be preferable to adapt some of the elaborate and varied preparation and consumption techniques developed in Argentina and Paraguay for *maté*—which, like cassina, derives from a species of *Ilex*—rather than borrowing techniques used with the Asian tea plant *Camellia sinensis.*[19]

Local use continued on a small scale, uninfluenced by this effort at development. In 1949 on the North Carolina coast and Outer Banks a "refreshing tea" was still made from the leaves and twigs of *Ilex vomitoria,* first parched in an oven (replacing an earlier method of placing them in a barrel under hot stones). The tea was flavored with a syrup containing lemon or orange juice or with cinnamon. It was said to be popular at Nags Head resorts.[20] By 1973 yaupon tea evidently was served only at the Pony Island Restaurant, Ocracoke Island, North Carolina, where it was recognized as a traditional local specialty. Here the leaves were parched in an oven with slow heat, then put in cold water and brought to a boil. After boiling about ten minutes, the tea was cooled and then poured off the leaves. It was served cold, or reheated, with sugar and lemon.[21]

Given the abundant evidence for Frenchmen drinking black drink with Louisiana Indians in the eighteenth century, French awareness of its use by the Spaniards in Florida, French interest in its supposed medicinal properties, and one report of a brief eighteenth-century introduction in Paris, it would not be surprising to find that *Ilex vomitoria* was taken into Louisiana French cuisine. But no evidence has so far been located for colonial French adoption of the beverage, aside from one 1716 report implying that it had been experimented with as a medicine. In the early twentieth century William A. Read searched unsuccessfully for its use among the Louisiana French.[22]

It is obvious from its caffeine content, from the nature of its uses, and from comparisons made by contemporary observers, that *Ilex vomitoria* as used by Euroamericans belongs both functionally and historically with a set of beverages that includes coffee, tea, chocolate, and *maté*. Modern European and Europe-derived cuisines have several very special structural or contextual positions for hot caffeine-containing beverages. All are similar in the value or importance placed on them, the specialized equipment for preparing, serving, and drinking them, the frequency with which they are drunk, the near-necessity of drinking one with breakfast and at the end of noon and evening meals, their use as a token of hospitality and to facilitate social intercourse, and their use at times other than meals, especially as a relaxant and, contradictorily, as a stimulant.

At present there are three such beverages, which vary in their popularity in comparable structural positions in different countries. Asian tea is primary, coffee secondary (but moving up), and chocolate a very poor third in Great Britain and in most British-derived overseas cultures. In the United States, coffee is primary, Asian tea secondary (and less important than coffee in Great Britain), and chocolate again a poor third. France ranks coffee first, Asian tea second (less important than in the U.S.A.), and then chocolate (probably more important than in the U.S.A.). In Spain, coffee has replaced chocolate in first position only over the last twenty or thirty years, while Asian tea is almost unknown. The same may be true of Mexico, although chocolate probably maintains its primary position there for nonurban people. In Russia, Asian tea is primary, and I suspect coffee and chocolate are less important than elsewhere in Europe. These varying usages are the results of a series of changes, many with an economic basis, over the last three hundred years.

Typically these beverages began their European careers as medicines or semi-medicinal beverages, then became luxuries for the aristocracy and the wealthy. Later they became commodities in the colonial trade and were commercialized in coffee houses for the urban middle classes. They then became subject both to taxation and to medical objections to their use. Finally they spread to the whole population and were incorporated into the ordinary cuisine. Chocolate participated only partially in this sequence of events, except in Spain. *Maté* never passed beyond medicinal experiments in Europe, but it became an object of commerce and a part of the cuisine in the Spanish colonies of southern South America. Cassina was of only very local interest, first as medicine and then as a primary beverage.

Chocolate was the first known of the caffeine-containing beverages and the earliest used in Europe. Discovered during the conquest of Mexico, Cortes mentioned it in his second letter on the conquest and in 1528 displayed it in Spain along with its usual Mexican equipment. Tea was first mentioned in print in Europe in 1559, in an Italian translation of a Persian traveler's account of China; and coffee was first mentioned in 1582, in a German traveler's description of Aleppo in 1573. Coffee drinking had spread through the Moslem Near East between about 1450 and 1550, and from there reached Venice by 1615, while tea (ancient in China and Japan) is said to have been first brought to Europe by the Dutch in 1606 (transshipped from Java) and was known in Portugal (from Japan, Formosa, or the East Indies) about the same time or somewhat earlier. Significant uses of coffee and tea in Europe lagged behind chocolate, which had spread from Spain to Florence by 1606, and by 1631 was reported to be known widely in Italy and Flanders and to be frequently used in Spain, especially in the court. In 1660 chocolate drinking was introduced to the French court by Marie-Thérèse, daughter of Philip IV of Spain, after her marriage to Louis XIV. But in all the countries of Europe except Spain, chocolate was soon superseded by coffee or tea in distribution and popularity. Coffee reached the Netherlands and England about 1637 and France about 1644; it was introduced to the court of Louis XIV in 1669 by the Turkish ambassador. Coffee houses became common in the Netherlands and England in the 1650s and 1660s and in Germany in the 1680s, and cafés became common in France in the 1670s and 1680s. Asian tea was well known, especially as a medicine, in the Netherlands in the late 1630s and was introduced from there to France about 1635 and to England around 1650. It was first sold publicly in England in 1657; and it was being used in the German courts by the same year, although in Germany its use was regarded as more effeminate than that of coffee or beer. Serious tea imports by the East India Company began in 1669, after the beverage had been introduced to the English aristocracy in 1662 through the marriage of the tea-drinking Portuguese Infanta Catherine to Charles II. Russia began to import tea overland from China in 1689. Tea as well as some chocolate was sold in England in what had already become known as coffee houses, and by 1700 tea was the normal beverage taken in these establishments. When Edmund Hickeringill wrote in 1705 "Bless the Mahometan Coffee, and the Popish Spanish Chocolate," he might well have added the Heathen Chinese Tea.

English coffee houses soon became literary and intellectual centers, as did the cafés of France, which, however, continued to specialize in their eponymous beverage—although tea had been taken up by the French court at least by the 1670s (where the idea of mixing it with milk is credited to Mme. de la Sablière in 1680). The number of coffee houses in London reached three thousand by 1700, but it took another fifty years before there were that many cafés in Paris. These English and French establishments were patronized mainly by men. In contrast, tea seems to have been served by women at home in the literary salons of France, and these soon became intellectual centers also. In England tea drinking at home or at "tea gardens" patronized by families was related to the decline of coffee houses in the second half of the eighteenth century.

By 1742 tea had replaced beer as the breakfast drink in ordinary English households; by 1750 nearly all Dutchmen also took tea with breakfast. Although coffee was said to be drunk daily by all classes in Germany by 1750, only in 1788 is it reported to have replaced soup as the usual breakfast drink in urban households. Even as late as 1825, neither coffee, tea, nor chocolate was a normal part of a Parisian breakfast.

Tea and coffee were introduced to the English colonies in America by William Penn in 1682, although the Dutch in New Amsterdam had been drinking tea before 1674. Tea is reported to have been first sold in Boston in 1690, and coffee in New York in 1696. By 1760 over one million pounds of tea per year were imported by the British North American colonies. However, the reaction against British tea taxes and the American Revolution which immediately followed led to a preference for coffee over tea in the United States. The boycott of English tea was lifted after the Revolution, but the final success of coffee in nineteenth-century America must be due to the long-term economic, if not patriotic, effects of the Revolution. To this day Canada continues to follow British custom in preferring tea over coffee.[23]

Maté fits the same chronology although not the same geographical distribution. Spaniards discovered it in use by the Guaraní Indians of Paraguay about 1540 and soon adopted it themselves in Paraguay and in northeastern Argentina. Indians suffered greatly from being forced to travel long distances to the lowland areas of the bordering regions of southern Brazil, eastern Paraguay, and northeastern Argentina, where the wild plant occurred, in order to collect and prepare the leaves for Spanish use in regions where the plant did not grow. Soon after the Jesuits established themselves in Paraguay in 1610, they began to specialize in the collection and export of the leaves, but they did not succeed in cultivating the plant until the early eighteenth century (and not until 1822 was *Ilex paraguariensis* first described adequately by a botanist). By the 1620s Spanish use of *maté* had spread as far as Chile, Bolivia, and Peru, and by 1750 it had reached the Ecuadorian Andes. At or somewhat before the expulsion of the Jesuits from Paraguay in 1768, they had introduced *maté* to Spain, Portugal, and Italy as a medicine against gallstones. Until about 1650 *maté* was regularly described as an emetic. Then preparation or consumption methods changed, so that use of the beverage, while continuing to be addictive or at least habit forming, no longer involved emesis. By the nineteenth and twentieth centuries, *maté*, prepared in a variety of ways, had become the national drink of Uruguay, Paraguay, southern Brazil, Argentina, and Chile.[24] One estimate for the mid-twentieth century put the number of people for whom *maté* was the principal beverage at fifteen million, as opposed to over three hundred million who used cocoa (which seems excessive and may include forms of consumption other than as a beverage). Half the total world population were tea drinkers, while one third of the world population were coffee drinkers.[25]

European adoption of these beverages evidently did not involve simple replacement of a native product by an exotic one, with consequent reorganization of the cuisine, as was the case with maize and "Irish" potatoes. Nor was it merely the addition of an exotic product to recipes already in use, as was the case with tomatoes and chile. Various beverages were of course part of European cuisines in the sixteenth century and before, but the structural position that came to be filled by the new caffeine-containing drinks apparently did not exist earlier. Miscellaneous herbal teas (compare the reference to sassafras in the 1595 quotation about St. Augustine), beer, mead, wine, distilled beverages, milk, broth, and water were in part displaced by the new drinks, but none of them had filled a comparable role.

That the potential existed for such a structural change is shown by the curious near simultaneity of adoption of chocolate, coffee, and tea by different European cultures, and also, more relevant to our present topic, by the fact that at about the same time European colonists in the New World adopted, for this structural slot, *maté* in southern South America and cassina in several places in southern North America. *Maté* has survived, but cassina was replaced by coffee and tea, just as coffee, tea, and chocolate were replaced by each other in different European cultures during the seventeenth and eighteenth centuries.

The question of why cassina has not survived and expanded is a complex one. Any satisfactory explanation of why coffee, tea, and chocolate came to be the preferred beverages among Europeans and Euroamericans and of why cassina and *maté* have had little importance for them will have to take account of many things, among them: (1) the pharmacological character of the beverages and their physiological effects, (2) the agricultural potential and adaptability of the plant sources, (3) the economics and politics of colonial exploitation of tropical products, (4) the overall structure of European cuisines and their relation to traditional medicine as well as to the organization of work and leisure, (5) the modes of cultural diffusion across European class and national boundaries; and (6) even chinoiserie and turcomania in seventeenth- and eighteenth-century Europe.

NOTES

1. Francisco Ximénez, *Cuatro libros de la naturaleza y virtudes de las plantas y animales, de uso medicinal en la Nueva España,* ed. Antonio Peñafiel (Mexico: Oficina Tip. de la Secretaría de Fomento, 1888) [first edition 1615], pp. 63–64.

2. Fray Andrés de San Miguel, "Relacion de los trabajos que la gente de una nao llamada Nra. Señora de la Merced padecio y de algunas cosas que en aquella flota sucedieron," in *Dos Antiguas relaciones de la Florida,* ed. Genaro García (Mexico: Tip. y Lit. de J. Aguilar Vera y Comp., 1902), pp. 196–97.

3. Jonathan Dickinson, *Jonathan Dickinson's Journal or, God's Protecting Providence . . . ,* ed. Evangeline Walker Andrews and Charles McLean Andrews (New Haven: Yale University Press, 1945), pp. 76–78, 90.

4. [Scribe], "Largos descargos y sentencias; residencia de Governador Jose de Zuñiga y Cerda, 7 de febrero, 1701." Manuscript in Archivo General de Indias, Seville, 58-2-8, cuaderno 4, p. 2946-38; photostat (filed under 1707) in Stetson Collection, University of Florida Library, Gainesville.

5. [Pedro de Rivera Márquez], *Continente americano, argonauta de las costas de Nueva España, y Tierra-Firme, islas, y baxos de esta navegacion, longitud, y altura de polo, de sus puertos, y noticias de estas habitaciones.* (Madrid?: no imprint, 1728?) [copy in Rare Book Division, Library of Congress, Washington, D.C.], pp. 2–3.

6. Thomas Ashe, "Carolina, or a Description of the Present State of that Country . . . 1682," in *Narratives of Early Carolina 1650–1708*, ed. Alexander S. Salley (New York: Charles Scribner's Sons, 1911) [pamphlet first published in 1682 in London], pp. 147–48.

7. [John Peachie], *Some Observations Made upon the Herb Cassiny; Imported from Carolina: Shewing its Admirable Virtues in Curing the Small Pox. Written by a Physitian in the Countrey to Esq; Boyle at London.* (London: no imprint, 1695). [Pamphlet of 8 pp.; Sir Joseph Banks's copy in the British Library, shelf-mark B.615.(13.).]

8. Johannes De Laet, *Novus Orbis seu descriptionis Indiæ Occidentalis libri XVIII* (Leiden: Elzevir, 1633), p. 217.

9. Samuel Purchas, *Purchas his Pilgrimage, or Relations of the World and the Religions Observed in all Ages and Places Discovered . . .* (London: William Stansby for Henrie Fetherstone, 1613), p. 644.

10. Verner W. Crane, *The Southern Frontier 1670–1732* (1929; reprint ed., Ann Arbor: University of Michigan Press, 1956), pp. 6–7, 13.

11. Mark Catesby, *The Natural History of Carolina, Florida and the Bahama Islands. . . .* (London: the author, 1731–1743), vol. 2, p. 57.

12. John Brickell, *The Natural History of North-Carolina. With an Account of the Trade, Manners, and Customs of the Christian and Indian Inhabitants . . .* (1737; rpt. ed., Raleigh: by authority of the Trustees of the public libraries, 1911), pp. 39, 58–59, 87–88. On Brickell's plagiarism of Lawson, and on the few additions he made from his own experience as a physician on the North Carolina coast in the 1730s, see Percy G. Adams, *Travelers and Travel Liars, 1660–1800* (Berkeley and Los Angeles: University of California Press, 1962), pp. 149–57.

13. Johann David Schöpf, *Reise durch einige der mittlern und südlichen Vereinigten nordamerikanischen Staaten . . .* (Erlangen: J. J. Palm, 1788), vol. 2, pp. 176–77; *Travels in the Confederation (1783–1784)*, trans. and ed. Alfred J. Morrison (Cleveland: Arthur H. Clark Co., 1911), vol. 2, pp. 113–14. No other mention of the commercial export of yaupon leaves to England has been located.

14. H. B. Croom, *A Catalogue of Plants, Native or Naturalized, in the Vicinity of New Bern, North Carolina, with Remarks and Syn-*

onyms (New York: G. P. Scott and Co., 1837), p. 45; Francis Peyre Porcher, *Resources of the Southern Fields and Forests, Medical, Economical, and Agricultural. Being also a Medical Botany of the Confederate States . . .* (Charleston: Evans and Cogswell, 1863), pp. 393–94 (Porcher may be mainly summarizing previous literature rather than reporting then-current folk usage; he does, however, include South Carolina as well as North Carolina among the regions using cassina tea); Henry M. Smith, "Yaupon," *Scientific American*, n.s., 26 (1872): 209; Frank G. Speck, "Remnants of the Machapunga Indians of North Carolina," *American Anthropologist* 18 (1916): 271–76 (see Merrill, this volume, on Speck's report).

15. E. M. Hale, *Ilex cassine, the Aboriginal North American Tea. Its History, Distribution, and Use among the Native North American Indians.* U.S.D.A. Division of Botany Bulletin no. 14 (Washington, D.C., 1891), p. 11; Porcher, *Resources,* loc. cit.

16. David Stick, *The Outer Banks of North Carolina 1584–1958* (Chapel Hill: University of North Carolina Press, 1958), pp. 177–78.

17. Roland M. Harper, *Economic Botany of Alabama, Part 2: Catalogue of the Trees, Shrubs and Vines of Alabama, with their Economic Properties and Local Distribution.* Geological Survey of Alabama Monograph no. 9 (University, Ala., 1928), p. 246. It was Harper who supplied samples of *Ilex vomitoria* in 1918 to Power and Chesnut (see note 18) for their chemical analyses for the U.S.D.A.

18. George F. Mitchell and J. W. Sale, "Beverages Produced from Cassina." Washington, D.C.: Bureau of Chemistry, U.S.D.A., [1923]. [Mimeographed; 4 pp.; copy in U.S.D.A. Library, Beltsville, Md.]; J. W. Sale and J. B. Wilson, "Manufacture of Concentrated Cassina Extract." Washington, D.C.: Water and Beverage Laboratory, Bureau of Chemistry, U.S.D.A., [1923]. [Mimeographed; 3 pp.; copy in U.S.D.A. Library, Beltsville, Md.]; Anonymous, "Page Sir Thomas Lipton," in *Industrial Bulletin of Arthur D. Little, Inc.* no. 48 (Cambridge, Mass., 1930); Anonymous, "The American Cassina Plant as the Source of a Table Beverage," Washington, D.C.: Bureau of Agricultural and Industrial Chemistry, Agricultural Research Administration, U.S.D.A., [1945?]. [Mimeographed; 3 pp.; copy in U.S.D.A. Library, Beltsville, Md.]; articles on this work are mentioned by Sale and Wilson as published in *The Spice Mill*, vol. 46, no. 3 (1923), p. 572, and *Tea and Coffee Trade Journal*, vol. 44, no. 3 (1923), pp. 348, 422. The recognition of the caffeine content of *Ilex vomitoria* was probably based on the study undertaken at the end of World War I by Frederick B. Power and Victor K. Chesnut, "Ilex vomitoria as a Native Source of Caffeine," *Journal of the American Chemical Society* 41 (1919): 1307–12.

19. *Maté* preparation techniques, utensils, and etiquette, especially

household ones, are described by Amaro Villanueva, *El mate: Arte de cebar*, 2d. ed. (Buenos Aires: Compañia General Fabril Editoria, 1960).

20. Dolores Butterfield Jeffords, "Carolina Tea-Time," *Nature Magazine* 42 (1949): 224–25.

21. Dicie Wells of Ocracoke, personal communication to William L. Merrill, May 14, 1973.

22. For French participation with the Indians see William L. Merrill's chapter in this volume. Pierre François Xavier de Charlevoix, *Journal of a Voyage to North-America . . . Containing the Geographical Description and Natural History of that Country . . ..* 2 vols. London: R. and J. Dodsley, 1761) [Translation of his *Histoire et description generale de la Nouvelle France . . .*, Paris, 1744.], 2: 305–6, repeats Ximénez's account of cassina in St. Augustine (without crediting his source), claims it is a good dissolvent, sudorific, and diuretic, and says "it began to be in some repute at Paris" before 1721. François Le Maire suggested in a letter from Mobile written May 13, 1718 (Archives Nationales, Paris, Marine, A S 4 67-1 [p. 11]; transcript in Manuscript Division, Library of Congress, Washington, D.C.) that the plant recently reported as in use in Paris was probably "le Paraguay," i.e. *maté*, from South America, rather than "le thé occidental ou Cassine" a medicinal plant of Louisiana. But Antoine de la Mothe Cadillac, governor of Louisiana, had sent a sample of *Ilex vomitoria*, "apalachine," to Paris in 1716, recommending it as a medicine to purify the blood, evacuate bile, and treat kidney stones, and as a diuretic, a pick-me-up, and to restore color to the complexion. He advised preparing it like coffee and drinking it hot, with a little sugar against its slight bitterness (Cadillac to the Council, January 23, 1716, Archives Nationales, Paris, Colonies, C13, A4, ff. 615–16; transcript in Manuscript Division, Library of Congress, Washington, D.C.). I am indebted to Mildred Mott Wedel for pointing out the Le Maire and Cadillac references. William A. Read's comments are on p. 85 of his "Louisiana French," *Louisiana State University Studies*, no. 5, (Baton Rouge, La., 1931).

23. Denys Forrest, *Tea for the British: The Social and Economic History of a Famous Trade* (London: Chatto and Windus, 1973), pp. 17–62; Alfred Franklin, *La Vie privée d'autrefois: arts et metiers, modes, moeurs, usages des Parisiens du XIIe au XVIIIe siècle d'après des documents originaux ou inédits.* [Tome 13:] *Le Café, le thé & le chocolat* (Paris: Librairie Plon, 1893), pp. 8–62, 122–49, 158–71; Percival Griffiths, *The History of the Indian Tea Industry* (London: Weidenfeld and Nicolson, 1967), pp. 15–21; Gervas Huxley, *Talking of Tea* (London: Thames and Hudson, 1956), pp. 10–79; Rodris Roth, "Tea Drinking in Eighteenth-Century America: Its Etiquette and Equipage," *Contributions from the Museum of History and Tech-*

nology, Paper No. 14, U.S. National Museum Bulletin 225, (Washington, D.C., 1961), pp. 61–91; Günther Schiedlausky, *Tee, Kaffee, Schokolade: Ihr Eintritt in die europäische Gesellschaft*. Bibliothek des germanischen National-Museums Nürnberg zur deutschen Kunstund Kulturgeschichte, vol. 17 (Munich, 1961), pp. 5–15; Otto F. Schleinkofer, *Der Tee*, 2d ed. (Hamburg: Cram, de Gruyter und Co., 1956), pp. 46–53; Boris P. Torgasheff, *China as a Tea Producer: Areas of Cultivation, Methods of Planting and Manufacture, Export Trade, Production and Consumption, Both in China and Abroad* (Shanghai: Commercial Press, 1926), pp. 148–51; William H. Ukers, *The Romance of Tea: An Outline History of Tea and Tea-drinking through Sixteen Hundred Years* (New York and London: Alfred A. Knopf, 1936), pp. 52–85; Frederick L. Wellman, *Coffee: Botany, Cultivation, and Utilization* (London: Leonard Hill, and New York: Interscience, 1961), pp. 16–25; Günter Wiegelmann, "Alltags- und Festspeisen; Wandel und gegenwärtige Stellung," *Atlas der Deutschen Volkskunde*, neue Folge, Beiheft 1 (Marburg, 1967), pp. 41, 165–67. The Hickeringill quotation is from James A. H. Murray et al., eds. *The Oxford English Dictionary*, 1933, *s.v.* chocolate.

24. Eduardo M. Grondona, "Historia de la yerba maté," *Revista Argentina de Agronomia* 20 (1953): 68–95, 21 (1954): 9–24; Victor Manuel Patiño, *Plantas cultivadas y animales domésticos en América Equinoccial. Tomo III: Fibras, medicinas, miscelaneas*, (Cali: Imprenta Departmental 1967), pp. 240–44; Amaro Villanueva, *El mate: Arte de cebar*, 1960.

25. Albert F. Hill, *Economic Botany: A Textbook of Useful Plants and Plant Products*, 2d ed. (New York: McGraw-Hill, 1952), p. 468.

Selected Bibliography

Abrams, H. Leon, Jr. "Caffeine—A Paradigm of Subliminal Cultural Drug Habituation." *Journal of Applied Nutrition* 28 (1976): 33–40.

Adair, James. *The History of the American Indians.* London, 1775.

Anonymous. "The American Cassina Plant as the Source of a Table Beverage." Mimeographed. Washington, D.C.: Bureau of Agricultural and Industrial Chemistry, Agricultural Research Administration, U.S.D.A., [1945?]. (Copy in U.S.D.A. Library, Beltsville, Md.)

Bartram, William. *The Travels of William Bartram.* Edited by Francis Harper. New Haven: Yale University Press, 1958.

Bossu, Jean-Bernard. *Jean-Bernard Bossu's Travels in the Interior of North America.* Edited and translated by Seymour Feiler. Norman: University of Oklahoma Press, 1962.

Burnett, E. K. "The Spiro Mound Collection in the Museum." Museum of the American Indian, Heye Foundation Contributions, no. 14, pp. 1–47. New York, 1945.

Cabeça de Vaca, Alvar Nuñez. *Relation of Alvar Nuñez Cabeça de Vaca.* Translated by Buckingham Smith. New York, 1871.

Cable, Harold; Hudson, Charles; and Merrill, William. "The Black Drink of the Southeastern Indians." Paper presented at the 1971 meeting of the American Society for Ethnohistory.

Dickinson, Jonathan. *Jonathan Dickinson's Journal or, God's Protecting Providence.* Edited by Evangeline W. Andrews and Charles M. Andrews. Philadelphia: Reinier Jansen, 1945.

Forrest, Denys. *Tea for the British: The Social and Economic History of a Famous Trade.* London: Chatto and Windus, 1973.

Gatschet, Albert S. *A Migration Legend of the Creek Indians,* 2 vols. Philadelphia, 1884.

Griffiths, Percival. *The History of the Indian Tea Industry.* London: Weidenfeld and Nicolson, 1967.

Grondona, Eduardo M. "Historia de la yerba mate." *Revista Argentina de Agronomia* 20 (1953): 68–95, 21 (1954): 9–24.

Hale, Edwin M. "Ilex cassine: The Aboriginal North American Tea." U.S.D.A. Division of Botany Bulletin no. 14. Washington, D.C., 1891.

Hawkins, Benjamin. "A Sketch of the Creek Country, in 1798 and '99." *Georgia Historical Society Collections,* vol. 3. Savannah, 1848.

Hudson, Charles. "Vomiting for Purity: Ritual Emesis in the Aboriginal Southeastern United States." In *Symbols and Society: Essays on Belief Systems in Action.* Edited by Carole Hill. Southern Anthropological Society Proceedings, no. 9. Athens: University of Georgia Press, 1975.

———. *The Southeastern Indians.* Knoxville: University of Tennessee Press, 1976.

Huxley, Gervas. *Talking of Tea.* London: Thames and Hudson, 1956.

Jeffords, Dolores Butterfield. "Carolina Tea-Time." *Nature Magazine* 42 (1949): 224–25.

Lawson, John. *A New Voyage to Carolina.* Edited by Hugh T. Lefler. Chapel Hill: University of North Carolina Press, 1967.

Le Moyne, Jacques. *Narrative of Le Moyne, An Artist Who Accompanied the French Expedition to Florida under Laudonnière, 1564.* Boston: James R. Osgood and Co., 1875.

Milfort, Louis Le Clerc. *Memoirs or A Quick Glance at my Various Travels and Sojourn in the Creek Nation.* Edited and translated by Ben C. McCary. Kennesaw, Ga.: Continental Book Co., 1959.

Mitchell, George F., and Sale, J. W. "Beverages Produced from Cassina." Mimeographed. Washington, D.C.: U.S.D.A. Bureau of Chemistry, [1923]. (Copy in U.S.D.A. Library, Belts-ville, Md.)

Peachie, John. *Some Observations Made upon the Herb Cas-siny; Imported from Carolina: Shewing its Admirable Virtues in Curing the Small Pox. Written by a Physitian in the Countrey to Esq; Boyle at London.* London: no imprint, 1695. (Pamphlet of 8 pp.; Sir Joseph Banks's copy in the British Library, shelf-mark B.615.[13.].)

Power, Frederick B., and Chestnut, Victor K. "Ilex vomitoria as a Native Source of Caffeine." *Journal of the American Chemical Society* 41 (1919): 1307–12.

Romans, Bernard. *A Concise History of East and West Florida.* Facsimile of the 1775 edition. Gainesville: University of Florida Press, 1962.

Roth, Rodris. *Tea Drinking in Eighteenth-Century America: Its Etiquette and Equipage.* Contributions from the Museum of History and Technology, Paper no. 14, U.S. National Museum Bulletin no. 225, pp. 61–91. Washington, D.C., 1961.

Sale, J. W., and Wilson, J. B. "Manufacture of Concentrated Cassina Extract." Mimeographed. Washington, D.C.: Water and Beverage Laboratory, U.S.D.A. Bureau of Chemistry [1923]. (Copy in U.S.D.A. Library, Beltsville, Md.)

Schiedlausky, Günther. *Tee, Kaffee, Schokolade: Ihr Eintritt in die europäische Gesellschaft.* Bibliothek des Germanischen National-Museums Nürnberg zur Deutschen Kunst- und Kulturgeschichte, vol. 17. Munich, 1961.

Schleinkofer, Otto F. *Der Tee.* 2d. ed. Hamburg: Cram, de Gruyter and Co., 1956.

Schultes, Richard Evans. "The Correct Name of the Yaupon." Botanical Museum Leaflets, Harvard University, vol. 14 no. 4. Cambridge, 1950.

Smith, Henry M. "Yaupon." *Scientific American,* n.s., 26 (1872): 209.

Swanton, John R. *Indian Tribes of the Lower Mississippi Valley and Adjacent Coast of the Gulf of Mexico.* Smithsonian

Institution, Bureau of American Ethnology Bulletin no. 43. Washington, D.C., 1911.

————. *Early History of the Creek Indians and Their Neighbors.* Smithsonian Institution, Bureau of American Ethnology Bulletin no. 73. Washington, D.C., 1922.

————. *Religious Beliefs and Medical Practices of the Creek Indians.* Smithsonian Institution, Bureau of American Ethnology Annual Report 42 (1928): 473–672.

————. *Social and Religious Beliefs and Usages of the Chickasaw Indians.* Smithsonian Institution, Bureau of American Ethnology Annual Report 44 (1928): 169–273.

————. *Source Material on the History and Ethnology of the Caddo Indians.* Smithsonian Institution, Bureau of American Ethnology Bulletin no. 132. Washington, D.C., 1942.

————. *The Indians of the Southeastern United States.* Smithsonian Institution, Bureau of American Ethnology Bulletin no. 137. Washington, D.C., 1946.

Torgasheff, Boris P. *China as a Tea Producer: Areas of Cultivation, Methods of Planting and Manufacture, Export Trade, Production and Consumption, Both in China and Abroad.* Shanghai: Commercial Press, 1926.

Ukers, William H. *The Romance of Tea: An Outline History of Tea and Tea-drinking through Sixteen Hundred Years.* New York and London: Alfred A. Knopf, 1936.

Villanueva, Amaro. *El mate: Arte de cebar.* 2d. ed. Buenos Aires: Compañía General Fabril Editora, 1960.

Waring, Antonio J., Jr. "The Southern Cult and Muskhogean Ceremonial." In *The Waring Papers,* edited by S. Williams, pp. 30–68. Athens: University of Georgia Press, 1968.

Waring, Antonio J., Jr., and Holder, Preston. "A Prehistoric Ceremonial Complex in the Southeastern United States." *American Anthropologist* 47 (1945): 1–34.

Wassen, S. H., ed. *A Medicine Man's Implements and Plants in a Tiahuanacoid Tomb in Highland Bolivia.* Etnologiska Studier 32. Göteborg: Göteborgs Etnografiska Museum, 1972.

Wellman, Frederick L. *Coffee: Botany, Cultivation, and Utilization*. London: Leonard Hill; New York: Interscience, 1961.

Witthoft, John. *Green Corn Ceremonialism in the Eastern Woodlands*. Occasional Contributions from the Museum of Anthropology of the University of Michigan, vol. 13, pp. 1–91. Ann Arbor, 1949.

The Contributors

CHARLES H. FAIRBANKS is Distinguished Service Professor of Anthropology at the University of Florida. He has done extensive work in the southeastern United States and is especially interested in historical archaeology.

SHIU YING HU is a botanist at the Arnold Arboretum, Harvard University. A specialist in Chinese plants and a world authority on the holly family (Aquifoliaceae), she has published over a hundred articles and several monographs. She is an authority on ginseng and other Chinese medicinal plants. Two of her recent books are *Wild Flowers of Hong Kong* (with B. M. Walden) and *The Genera of Orchidaceae of Hong Kong*.

CHARLES HUDSON is professor of anthropology at the University of Georgia. He has done research on comparative belief systems and the culture and history of the Indians of the southeastern United States. He is editor of *Red, White, and Black: Symposium on Indians in the Old South* and *Four Centuries of Southern Indians* and the author of *The Catawba Nation* and *The Southeastern Indians*.

WILLIAM L. MERRILL is a doctoral candidate in anthropology at the University of Michigan, Ann Arbor. His research interests include world view, religion, and ethnobotany with particular emphasis on the use of psychotropic plant substances. He is currently involved in a field investigation of the world view of the Tarahumara Indians of Chihuahua, Mexico.

JERALD T. MILANICH is associate curator in archaeology at the Florida State Museum, Gainesville, and editor of *The Florida Anthropologist*. He has concentrated his ethnohistorical and archaeological research on the aboriginal peoples of Florida and Georgia.

WILLIAM C. STURTEVANT is curator of North American ethnology at the Smithsonian Institution, Washington. He has conducted ethnographic fieldwork among the Florida Seminole and elsewhere, and he has done research on Eastern North American Indian ethnohistory, on several topics in historical ethnobotany, and on the history of cultural interchanges between Amerindians and Europeans.

Index

CPSIA information can be obtained
at www.ICGtesting.com
Printed in the USA
LVHW031808140319
610673LV00001B/95